GOD
STILL
MAKES
SENSE

GOD STILL MAKES SENSE

BEN M. HERBSTER

United Church Press
New York

Unless otherwise indicated, the scripture quotations are from
the Revised Standard Version of the Bible, copyright 1946, 1952 by
the Division of Christian Education of the National Council of the
Churches of Christ in the U.S.A. and are used by permission. Scripture
quotations marked NEB are from *The New English Bible,* © The
Delegates of the Oxford University Press and the Syndics of the Cam-
bridge University Press 1961. Reprinted by permission.

This book is printed on acid-free, recycled paper.

To Elizabeth, Jane, and Anne,
without whom my life
would be poor indeed

CONTENTS

PREFACE

As I look out upon the church today I have one consuming concern, and it is that to which I will address myself. Of course, concern for the church is nothing new. In every age, in every circumstance, in every country where people love God and are involved in the mission, concern for the church is a continuing attitude. Because of the command of our Lord, the desires of our heart can never fully be expressed in the life of the church. Troubled by the wide divergence between what the church ought to be, what we want the church to be, and what she is, concern is inevitable. The church is made up of people like us, and we always fall short of our best and of God's best in us.

The thing which concerns me at the moment, however, is the fact that many of us feel so compelled to be out in the world where the needs of men are so apparent (and I have no quarrel with this) that we have little or no time at all to continue the cultivation of our own spiritual life and our own closeness to our Creator and the Lord of our Life. As I get about the church, I see expressed in so many places and in so many ways what seems to me a misconception: that if we are busy serving the needs of our fellowmen, that is enough; that somehow almost by magic our love for God will be increased and our understanding of God—his great love for us, his great deeds, his great dream for the world—will possess us. The longer I

9

live, the more I come to see that this is not true. Understanding of God—with all that means—comes only to those who devote some of their time, some of their energy, some of their life to nurturing that understanding. It also follows logically that before one is equipped to go out on the mission to help meet the needs of the world, one ought to know, to understand, to love, to be devoted to the God who loves us. How can we know what he would have us do unless we know him!

Now, lest you misunderstand what I am writing about, let me quickly add that when I say we must know God before we can serve him, I am not writing about a chronological order, but a logical one. That is, you do not spend the first half of your life learning about God and then somewhere about the age of thirty-five or forty years begin to serve him. The learning experience and the serving experience go hand in hand. One learns by serving and one serves by learning. Some of the most valuable learning experiences are those that one has as he serves. But it is also true that unless one has some knowledge, one's service is not likely to be of worth, either to God or to men.

With this concern uppermost in my mind and out of this background, I began, a few years ago, to preach some sermons on the ways in which God reveals himself to men, about the ways in which men can learn about God. Notice the plural of the noun ways. There is no one road alone that leads in this direction. There are many roads, and those many roads we need to travel.

The chapters of this book have as their purpose the outlining of these ways, so that a person can know, if he really wants to, what God is like, the direction which he is going, and therefore the direction in which we are to go after him. The longer I have studied this need of the church, the more I have come to see the importance of this emphasis.

Yet very quickly, and with no less emphasis, would I add that when we know something about God and the direction in which he is leading, it is also important for us then to commit ourselves—time, talent, and resources —to going with him, out into the world to help make the world "new" and better. The person who knows more about God than any of his contemporaries, but then lives as if he had no responsibility to the world, to mission, to his brothers, has missed the mark. It is not either one to the exclusion of the other, but both as complementary parts of one whole.

The emphasis of this book is such as it is because at the moment I see this as one of the great weaknesses of all our emphasis upon social action.

PART I
GOD

CHAPTER 1
GOD—
WHO
IS HE?

Who is God? What is he like? How can we know about
him? How does he reveal himself to us? What are the
ways we must travel, the directions in which we must go
so that he will not be some nebulous spirit in some far-off
blue yonder, but will be real to us as we live our everyday
life and as we seek to make that life count for him and
his cause?

There are two great periods in the church year, Advent and Lent. Advent means "the coming." The very
word signifies the importance of the event which we celebrate and for which we make our hearts ready during the
Advent days. Our attention is mobilized by the words in
the prophecy of Isaiah: "Prepare ye the way of the Lord,
make straight in the desert a highway for our God. Every
valley shall be exalted and every mountain and hill shall
be made low: and the crooked shall be made straight, and
the rough places plain (40:3-4, KJV)." John the Baptist
quotes these words as a call to the people of his day to
make themselves ready for God's Anointed.

There are also the words of the angel to Mary:

Hail, O favored one, the Lord is with you! . . . Do
not be afraid, Mary, for you have found favor with
God. And behold, you will conceive in your womb
and bear a son, and you shall call his name Jesus.

He will be great, and will be called the Son of
the Most High;
and the Lord God will give to him the throne
of his father David,
and he will reign over the house of Jacob for
ever;
and of his kingdom there will be no end.

—Luke 1:28, 30-33

And there are also those words which are still more beautiful, poured forth from the lips of the angel who had come to announce "the coming" to the shepherds:

"Be not afraid; for behold, I bring you good news
of a great joy which will come to all the people;
for to you is born this day in the city of David, a
Savior, who is Christ the Lord. And this will be a
sign for you: you will find a babe wrapped in
swaddling cloths and lying in a manger." And suddenly there was with the angel a multitude of the
heavenly host praising God and saying,
"Glory to God in the highest,
and on earth peace among men with whom he is
pleased!"

—Luke 2:10-14

But the significance of Advent stems not from the glory of the angels or the beauty of the words or the wonder of the message. The significance of Advent comes rather from who it was that was visiting the world. Biblical background for this is to be found in the prologue of the Gospel of John (1:14): "And the Word became flesh and dwelt among us, full of grace and truth; we have beheld his glory, glory as of the only Son from the Father." Alongside these words, I would like to put a couple of sentences which are to be found in the Statement of Faith

16

of the United Church of Christ. If you are at all familiar with that statement you will remember that it begins, "We believe in God the Eternal Spirit, Father of our Lord Jesus Christ and our Father and to his deeds we testify." And then halfway down in the statement is one of these great deeds to which we give testimony: "In Jesus Christ, the man of Nazareth, our crucified and risen Lord, he [God] has come to us and shared our common lot, conquering sin and death and reconciling the world to himself." J. B. Phillips, in his book *God Our Contemporary* writes:

> Christianity begins with an historical fact. Indeed its starting point is the most important event in the whole of human history. The Christian religion asserts that nearly two thousand years ago, God, whose vast and complex wisdom scientists are daily uncovering, visited this planet in person. Naturally, the only way he could do this was by becoming a human being. And this is precisely what Christians believe he did. This is the heart and the center of the Christian faith. This is the gospel of good news which those who had witnessed this extraordinary event went out to tell the world.*

I must confess that for a long time I had trouble with the prologue of the Gospel of John, trying to understand it and to lay it bare so others could understand it. Now I am sure that my trouble was that I was trying too hard. Perhaps it was a verse out of the great drama of Job that helped me to see what really was being set forth; that and our Statement of Faith. First, Job. You recall the setting? Job had been troubled with what he believed was more

---

* J. B. Phillips, *God Our Contemporary* (New York: Macmillan, 1960), p. 52. Used by permission.

than his fair share of difficulty. He lost his property, he lost his sons and daughters, then boils infected his body, and his wife turned on him. Finally, his best friend came, supposedly to comfort him but really to tell him that his suffering so much trouble was definite proof that, more than others, he had been a sinner. This Job could not take, for his conscience was clear, and he cried out:

> Oh, that I knew where I might find him,
>   that I might come even to his seat! . . .
> [and] lay my case before him
>   and fill my mouth with arguments.
>   —Job 23:3-4

Isn't that a wonderful scene? So natural, so human, so much like what we would feel. If I could only find God I would tell him a thing or two!

And then finally the drama proceeds with God's coming to Job. The interesting thing is that then Job has not one word to say. You ought to reread the thirty-eighth, thirty-ninth, fortieth, and forty-first chapters of Job. They are really superb as they set forth the works of God and every so often ask whether Job has contemplated them. After Job has tried in vain to answer the questions God puts to him and has not one word to say (this one who was going to back God into a corner in order to question him), he finally says,

> I had heard of thee by the hearing of the ear,
>   but now my eye sees thee;
> therefore I despise myself,
>   and repent in dust and ashes.
>   —Job 42:5-6

"I had heard of thee by the hearing of the ear." He had read and understood the long history of the universe as it was written in words. You see, up to the time of

Christ religion was only words. It was all in words, and when one speaks words there is so much chance of misunderstanding. I must confess to you that I always have trouble reading the directions for assembling any piece of machinery. They are always explicit—in fact, they are sometimes overexplicit (or else I am stupid). Words are hard to understand and easy to misinterpret. All through the Old Testament, God had been speaking words through the patriarchs, the prophets, the poets. The words which God had spoken were important, very important, but men had a hard time understanding them. Some of this misunderstanding was feigned by those who did not want to hear, but some of it was sincere. It is always easy to misunderstand spoken or written instructions.

"When the time had fully come, God sent forth his Son, born of woman, born under the law, to redeem those who were under the law, so that we might receive adoption as sons (Gal. 4:4-5)." In the fullness of time God moved to change the written and the spoken word into a man—a baby, a lad, a man—so that what men had not been able to get straight and understand through the word and the voice, now they could understand because this man lived and walked among them and they could see. J. B. Phillips translates this as "The Word became a human being and lived among us (John 1:14)."* Well, that is the miracle that happened at Christmas. When men wanted to know about God, what he was like, they no longer had to wonder or search the scriptures or listen. Now they could see, for Jesus was and is and evermore shall be, God in human form—all of God that can be crammed into a human body. The word, the word about God, about life, about love, about men, the Word made flesh. "The word became a human being, a man," "the

---

* J. B. Phillips, *The New Testament in Modern English* (New York: Macmillan, 1962), p. 186.

Man," Pilate said later. Men began to understand what God was like because they could see him.

This is what the writers of the Statement of Faith were trying to say: "We believe in God the eternal Spirit, Father of our Lord Jesus Christ and our Father, and to his [God's] deeds we testify." "In Jesus Christ the man of Nazareth our crucified and risen Lord he [God] has come to us and shared our common lot, conquering sin and death and reconciling the world to himself." The coming of Jesus was God's act so that men would no longer have to wonder whether they were reading the word correctly or not. Now they could see him. That is what is said in John 1:14. This has but one great meaning: if you want to know something about God, you look at Jesus Christ. God broke into life in Jesus Christ.

Now, when people look at Jesus and through him to God, what do they see? First, they see a man who was totally committed to righteousness, justice, and holiness. And that was really something new in the world—and it is still unique today. The lengths to which we go to justify what we do—when deep within our hearts we know that it is not up to our standards, the standards which we expect others to meet—are beyond imagining. "Everybody else is doing it, why shouldn't I?" "No one will find out anyway." "It's old-fashioned!" "Even God does not expect me to walk the hard and straight way." You know how we talk when we try to justify our crooked ways. But here was one, come into the world to reveal what God is like—and he was different. He was righteous all the way through. He was holy in a way no one else has ever been holy, before or since. The Hebrews seeing him and hearing him said, "He taught them as one who had authority, and not as their scribes (Matt. 7:29)"—the authority of integrity. No one accused him of not living up to his preachments. He embodied the words he spoke in the life he lived. That is why he made such an impression upon the people, upon his day, upon us even in this confused and bewildered age. Here was one who was true to that for which he stood—that for which God stands. I wish it were possible for me to shout out so that all could hear the words about God that Abraham uttered five thousand years ago. He put it in the form of a question—a rhetorical question. "Shall not the Judge of all the earth do right? (Gen. 18:25) " There is no argument about that. If God is God, then his ways are holy and his thoughts are pure, and his plans for the universe are just and perfect. And then remember the words of our Lord, "You, therefore, must be perfect, as your heavenly Father is perfect. (Matt. 5:48) " Righteous, holy, just, clear through—as Paul speaks about the church, "without spot or blemish or wrinkle or anything that will mar. (Eph. 5:27) "

That brings me to a corollary to all this. The one thing that Christ, and presumably God, cannot stomach is a great front of right doing which is not backed up by the everyday acts of holiness. This was what he was always crying out, criticizing the scribes and the Pharisees because their deeds did not conform to the way they talked. Listen to him: "Woe to you, scribes and Pharisees, hypocrites! for you tithe mint and dill and cummin, and have neglected the weightier matters of the law, justice and mercy and faith; these you ought to have done, without neglecting the others (Matt. 23:23) " (or, as one of the modern translators puts it, "you tithe in your garden down to the last mint leaf"). Do you get the imagery? Here are the religious leaders, the elite of the church, those people who pretended to be somebody. Yet as he looked upon their hearts Jesus saw that their deeds and their hearts did not correspond. They were interested only in a great show. Jesus said deeds grow out of attitudes, and therefore attitudes are important. This is the reason why Jesus never made any distinction between various kinds of evilness, never indicated that a particular sin was of less concern than others. For he saw that anything that was evil was disobedience to God and his way of life, and therefore wrong—expressing a wrong relationship between a man and his God. I heard a great teacher say it this way: "If you are going to fight sin, you have to do it in the imagination stage." That is what these Pharisees never did—and what so many times we fail to do. In the King James Version we read in Proverbs 23:7 "As [a man] thinketh in his heart, so is he." Integrity—that is what Jesus portrayed, what he stood for, the way he lived; and he expects us to live like that too.

In the second place, when they looked at Jesus they saw behind him and through him a God for whom people are important, more important than anything else in the world. For God, the measure of any act or any thought was what effect it had on people, on a single person. Now, that is a foreign idea to the way of the world, to the way so many people live in this generation. The measure of what we do is usually what effect it has on us: whether we get ahead doing it, whether it is good for us. But not so for God and the Son whom he sent. What it did to people and for people—for the individual—was the measure of its rightness or wrongness. And you do not find this criterion anyplace else except in the Hebrew Christian faith. It is interesting to note that in the Old Testament God is not revealed as the God of mankind in the mass, but the God of Abraham, of Isaac and Jacob. God does not lump us all together; each of us is known to him by his own name. I cannot tell you how that is; I can only say that so it is revealed in the word.

Part of our trouble in understanding stems from the fact that we have a hard time keeping everybody sorted out, and therefore we think God must be plagued by that same trouble. As a little aside, let me say that there are, you know, two million members in the United Church of Christ. Almost every Sunday I was out preaching somewhere, and in the course of those visits I met a lot of people. When I would meet them again later on, under different circumstances and in different places, some of them expected me to be able to call them by name.

Well, the difficulty we have leads us to assume that God too has trouble keeping us all straight. But the Book does not say that. And the life of our Lord does not reveal that. He knew his own. He understood their problems. The woman at the well of Samaria went away and said, "Come, see a man who told me all that I ever did (John 4:29)." When he saw Nathaniel—whom he had never laid eyes on before—he said, "Behold, an Israelite indeed, in whom is no guile (John 1:47)!" About a child he said pointedly, "But whoever causes one of these little ones who believe in me to sin, it would be better for him to have a great millstone fastened round his neck and to be drowned in the depth of the sea (Matt. 18:6)." He said whosoever traded his life for the whole world had made a bad bargain. Do you recall the words: "For what will it profit a man, if he gains the whole world and forfeits his life? Or what shall a man give in return for his life (Matt. 16:26)?" To create man and help him live in God's own image was and is and ever shall be the purpose of all this universe, of all this creating process. Edwin Markham puts it this way:

> We are all blind until we see
> That in the human plan [and it would be much
>   more accurate to say "In God's plan for hu-
>   mans"]
> Nothing is worth the making
> If it does not make the man.
>
> Why build these cities glorious
> If man unbuilded goes?
> In vain we build the work, unless
> The builder also grows.*

---

* Edwin Markham, "Man-Making." Reprinted by permission of Virgil Markham.

Jesus, reflecting God's care for the individual man or woman or child, was always concerned about them; he was always seeing them, and always his heart was moved with compassion for them. He was always stopping to lift the fallen, to give hope to the despairing, to heal the broken and the brokenhearted, to release the captive, and to restore sight to the blind. He was never too busy to serve the needs of a man who was in distress. And he did all this because God, his Father, and ours, is also that kind of a God.

In the third place, Jesus came from God as a gift of love because the Father loves us. One of the most poignant paragraphs in the Old Testament is where Israel is compared to a child whom God is teaching to walk. Can you remember back to the days when your youngster took his first steps? How exciting it was, how concerned you were? Well, for God, the prophet sets the stage:

> When Israel was a child, I loved him,
>   and out of Egypt I called my son.
> The more I called them,
>   the more they went from me;
> they kept sacrificing to the Baals,
>   and burning incense to idols.
> Yet it was I who taught Ephraim to walk
>   I took them up in my arms;
>   but they did not know that I healed them.
> I led them with cords of compassion,
>   with the bands of love.
> and I became to them as one
>   who eases the yoke on their jaws,
>   and I bent down to them and fed them.
>   —Hosea 11:1-4

It seems to me that this picture makes more plain what we have heard so often. "As a father pities his children, so the Lord pities those who fear him," even those

24

who never seem to take the time to acknowledge him. How familiar are the words "For God is love—in this is love, not that we loved God but that he loved us and sent his Son to be the expiation for our sins (1 John 4:10)." "For God so loved the world that he gave his only Son, that whoever believes in him should not perish but have eternal life." Note the word whoever. There is an old gospel hymn that expresses the truth: "When the Lord said 'whosoever' he included me." A generation ago the great missionary to India, E. Stanley Jones, wrote, "The greatest news that has ever been broken to the human race is the news that God is like Jesus." He goes on, "I have watched the look of incredulity come to the faces of men in India as the announcement is made but incredulity gives way to the thought that God ought to be like that and that in turn to the thought that he is." This is exactly what we read in this prologue to the Gospel of John (1:18) : "No one has ever seen God; the only Son, who is in the bosom of the Father, he has made him known." In *The New English Bible* this is translated "No one has ever seen God; but God's only Son, he who is nearest to the Father's heart, he has made him known." And, above everything else and beyond everything else he has made him known as love. "See what love the Father has given us, that we should be called children of God; and so we are (1 John 3:1)." When you look at Jesus then you know, perhaps for the first time, something about the love with which God loves us.

In the catechism in which I was reared, the first question is: "What is thy only comfort in life and in death." And the answer: "That I with body and soul, both in life and in death, am not my own but belong to my faithful Savior Jesus Christ." Not our own, for he has loved us; and from that love we learn about the great love of the Father for us. Jesus came to reveal the Father as a God of love.

We sometimes wonder why Advent days have a different spirit from those of the rest of the year. Wonder no more—it is because of who it is who comes into the world at Christmas. We sing it with great gladness, but sometimes we fail to understand the meaning of the words:

> Joy to the world! the Lord is come:
> Let earth receive her King.

"In Jesus Christ, the man of Nazareth our crucified and risen Lord, he [God] has come to us and shared our common lot, conquering sin and death and reconciling the world unto himself." "It was God in Christ reconciling the world to himself." It is God in the flesh—all of God that you can cram into a man, whom we greet at Christmas, so that no longer do we have to wonder what God is like. All we have to do is to look at Jesus and then we know. For the word (all this talk and writing about God) became in Jesus flesh—the flesh of a human, and then we beheld his glory full of grace and truth. Thank God the Lord is come.

CHAPTER 2
GOD
AS
SAVIOR

The texts—for there are several of them—all set forth the fact that this one, who was all of God that could be crammed into a man, is Savior. It was for this cause that he came into the world. First, from the first chapter of Matthew, where the angel was speaking to Joseph about the child which Mary was to bear: "She will bear a son, and you shall call his name Jesus, for he will save his people from their sins." The second is from the second chapter of Luke, from the message of the angel to the shepherds: "For to you is born this day in the city of David a Savior, who is Christ the Lord." Or the words of Simeon when Mary and Joseph took Jesus into the temple at the time of the purification of Mary. The old man held the babe in his arms and said,

> Lord, now lettest thou thy servant depart in peace,
> according to thy word;
> for mine eyes have seen thy salvation
> which thou hast prepared in the presence of all
> peoples,
> a light for revelation to the Gentiles,
> and for glory to thy people Israel.
>
> —Luke 2:29-32

Or the words which Jesus himself spoke when, on the first sabbath of his ministry, he went into the synagogue in Nazareth; when asked to read the lesson, he read from Isaiah, as a sort of an inaugural:

The Spirit of the Lord God is upon me,
　　because the Lord has anointed me
to bring good tidings to the afflicted;
　　he has sent me to bind up the brokenhearted,
to proclaim liberty to the captives,
　　and the opening of the prison to those who are
　　　　bound;
to proclaim the year of the Lord's favor.
　　　　　　　　　　　　　　　　　　—Isaiah 61:1-2

Or again at a later time: "No one comes to the Father, but by me (John 14:6)." These and other sentences from the Word which I could repeat to you are more than enough to convince us that God sent his Son to be Savior of the world, that through him we might have eternal life. The one who came into the world, for whose coming we prepare ourselves in the Advent season, was and is and ever shall be Savior.

Now, the fact that God came as Savior presupposes that men need a Savior. In a way, one ought to be able to take that for granted; but there is so much that points in a different direction. We are not always as conscious of sin as we ought to be—and of what sin really is. There is so much in our day that makes us proud and forgetful of by whose strength we live and move and have our being. We have a way of thinking we can do anything. And we can do a lot. Certainly I have long since quit saying that something or other will never be done; for while one is talking, someone else has gone ahead and done it. We have explored outer space, we have plumbed the depths of the ocean, we have harnessed the power of the atom, we have found specific cures for many of our more dreaded diseases. Perhaps it is no wonder that we believe ourselves equal or more than equal to God. And that is just where the trap is. That, in fact, is the essence of sin. Trying to push God out of the central place in his universe and establishing ourselves, trying to enthrone ourselves in his place.

I do not know whether you have noticed that I invariably use the word sin, in the singular and not the plural. Sins are not primarily my concern. My concern is with sin —the attitude of heart and mind that sets itself against God, that does not want to accept the subordination that always belongs to the creature in relationship with the Creator. Out of that wrong relationship come the sins (what we do and say that is against the will of God). You find this striving to be equal with God or superior to him in the very beginning of the Book. In the third chapter of Genesis the serpent says to Eve:

Did God say, "You shall not eat of any tree of the garden"? And the woman said to the serpent, "We may eat of the fruit of the trees of the garden; but God said, 'You shall not eat of the fruit of the tree which is in the midst of the garden, neither shall you touch it, lest you die.' " But the serpent said to the woman, "You will not die. For God knows that when you eat of it your eyes will be opened, and you will be like God, knowing good and evil."

Observe the striving to be like God here. That is just what men have wanted: to do anything anytime they wanted, without getting the permission of anyone. This is what God cries out against. In Isaiah 29:13 it is recorded:

Because this people draw near with their mouth
    and honor me with their lips.
    while their hearts are far from me,
and their fear of me is a commandment of men
    learned by rote.

What God wants, what he must have is the love of our

hearts—and then the deeds we do will all fall into line. "You shall love the Lord your God with all your heart, and with all your soul, and with all your mind. This is the great and first commandment. And a second is like it, You shall love your neighbor as yourself (Luke 22:37-39)."

By this standard, who of us can stand foursquare before the Lord? Sin, disobedience, is so much with us that we cannot extricate ourselves from it. It is like lifting ourselves with our own boot straps—perhaps for people who do not remember boot straps we should say it is like standing on a piece of paper and trying to get it out from under our own feet. As he contemplated his own life, Paul, who certainly in righteousness and doing the will of God exceeded most of us, said, "For I do not do the good I want, but the evil I do not want is what I do. . . . Who will deliver me from this body of death (Rom. 7:19, 24)?" And yet he more than others knew the answer to the question which he raised. God in Christ will separate him from the treason, the treachery of his own life. God came into the world as Savior.

But the sin that is so much a part of us does not only consist (and primarily so) of this individual compulsion to rebel against God; we are also a part of a society that is pagan from beginning to end. This does not mean that there is nothing good in our world, but it does mean that there is so much evil, and the evil makes so much noise, that sometimes one has to take a second or third or fourth look to find the good. And the truth of the matter is that we cannot disentangle ourselves from the guilt of this sin, even when we would. A few acquaintances of mine think they can be free of the guilt of war, simply by refusing to pay that part of their income tax which goes to the support of war. Now, the truth is that life is not nearly that simple. Every day these same people enjoy the fruits of an economy which is supported, in no little measure, by the whole war machine. Many of these people have jobs which, though having no direct relationship to the making of war, would not exist if it were not for the war economy. What I mean to say is that one cannot separate oneself from the results, the guilt of the whole war enterprise.

So it is with other facets of this same problem. I say humbly, but not without some fact, that I believe I am as unprejudiced racially as a white can be—and yet I live in a society which is racist and for which, therefore, I bear more than a little responsibility, even though I work, stand, and support efforts toward an unprejudiced society, a society where every man has dignity and worth to himself and his fellows. No matter how much I strive toward such an end, I am a part of a society that discriminates, that is prejudiced, and that is unjust. Therefore I partly am responsible; I bear the unmistakable marks of some of the guilt of society. It is inevitable that this be so. The question often arises as to why Jesus was baptized for the remission of sins if he was sinless. I suppose there are many answers. He did it for an example, so that we should follow in that same course. But partly, I am certain, he was baptized because of the sin of society of which he was part. And don't forget it was sinful, just as our society is not without fault. No matter how perfect Jesus was individually, he could not entirely escape the responsibility for the sin of society. Therefore, as an indication of his oneness with all mankind in mankind's disobedience, he suffered himself to be baptized.

Is this enough to firmly establish in your mind the need for a Savior? Well, that Savior came to earth in the form of a babe, lived through adolescence into manhood, taught, healed, preached, lived as no man has ever lived, and then at long last, according to the plan of God, went to the cross in order that on that cross he might work for man his reconciliation with God. That is what the word

31

of the precious sixteenth verse of John 3 means: "For God so loved the world that he gave his only Son, that whoever believes in him should not perish but have eternal life. For God sent the Son into the world, not to condemn the world, but that the world might be saved through him." Or remember the words of Paul that "Christ Jesus came into the world to save sinners. And I am the foremost (1 Tim. 1:15)." Or that Jesus himself said; "For the Son of man came to seek and to save the lost (Matt. 18:11)." I believe I never say that word lost but there comes over me a sense of grief and agony which I am not able to shake off. It is a terrifying thing to be lost. If you want to know how terrifying, observe some little child who becomes separated from his mother in a crowd. There you have it in stark, unmistakable lines. The brokenness, the fear, the anxiety of that child is beyond description—but you understand it. It is that word that Jesus says he has come to change. Lost, lostness. "For the Son of man came to seek and to save the lost." And without him all of us are lost. He said, "Those who are well have no need of a physician, but those who are sick (Matt. 9:12)." And all of us are sick, sick with an illness of the soul.

Now, the next question is: How is it that the birth of a baby, the growth of that baby into manhood, his ministry, and—supremely—his death and resurrection bring life where only death existed? Why and how is there hope in him? First of all, let me say very frankly that a complete answer to that cannot be given. I do not know fully how one man can take upon himself the sin and the guilt for all the world. I do not know how it is that when that man was lifted high upon a cross, those who look to him find new life and a new beginning. Actually, the ways of God are very strange and at best inexplicable. But this I do know. That in the year A.D. 30 and in every year since that time this has been the experience of men. This is

32

nothing like a philosophy or a theology that is spun out of the convolutions of a man's head but has no counterpart in the experience of men. This is what has brought, and is bringing, and will yet bring hope and forgiveness and reconciliation to men. It is as the writer of the Gospel of John expressed it: "And as Moses lifted up the serpent in the wilderness, so must the Son of man be lifted up, that whoever believes in him may have eternal life (John 3:14-15)."

You know that story. The children of Israel had rebelled against the Lord and had charged that Moses had brought them out into the wilderness to die. Now, you have to remember that every day along the way God had cared for them in miraculous ways. But here they were complaining again. And so, as the story goes, God sent serpents among the people of Israel, and many died. Then the people returned to Moses and said:

> "We have sinned, for we have spoken against the Lord and against you; pray to the Lord, that he take away the serpents from us." So Moses prayed for the people. And the Lord said to Moses, "Make a fiery serpent, and set it on a pole; and every one who is bitten, when he sees it, shall live." So Moses made a bronze serpent, and set it on a pole; and if a serpent bit any man, he would look at the bronze serpent and live.
>
> —Numbers 21:7-9

Well, this is the background of what Jesus says in the third chapter of John: "And as Moses lifted up the serpent in the wilderness, so must the Son of man be lifted up."

The point of all this is that a diagram of how it works cannot be drawn. But the fact is written in history. I can only look within my own life; I can only report what has

33

been the experience of others. They, we, anyone who looks to Christ in faith finds that his sin is forgiven, that he has a new chance, that he does become a new creation in Christ Jesus. That does not mean that never again does he sin, that never again does he make a mistake, that never again is he rebellious. But this wall of separation that men have built to shut God out is no longer there, and he feels restored to the Father's heart and home. And what a change, what a relief, what a joy is this! It is as it is with the little child who is lost and then finds his mother. Lostness is terrible—but foundness is joy unspeakable.

There is a hymn with which you may be familiar. The words are wonderful and have point just here, expressing what has been written.

> I know not how that Bethlehem's babe
> Could in the Godhead be;
> I only know the manger child
> Has brought God's life to me.
>
> I know not how that Calvary's cross
> A world from sin could free;
> I only know its matchless love
> Has brought God's love to me.
>
> I know not how that Joseph's tomb
> Could solve death's mystery;
> I only know a living Christ,
> Our immortality.

That is it. The thing works. It passes the pragmatic test. And it has been doing that for two thousand years. And you do not have to draw a diagram about it, you do not have to explain it, to be blessed by it. It is like eating. If you had to wait until you prove how food that is taken into the mouth is digested in the stomach and absorbed

34

into the blood and becomes muscle, sinew, and energy before you could partake of your first meal, you would not live long enough even to begin the study. The thing works, and that is what is important to you. At Christmas God breaks into his world in order to be the Savior of his people. In order that through Christ the sinner (and all of us are sinners) can be brought home again. In order that the lost shall be found. "For to you is born this day . . . a Savior, who is Christ the Lord."

Is it any wonder that this story is called the gospel, for gospel means good news, and this is good news certainly! There is hope and there can be joy, and there is forgiveness and a new chance.

CHAPTER 3
GOD
HAS COME
TO US—LIFE

"And the Word became flesh and dwelt among us (John 1:14)." Why? So that God might reveal himself to us in terms of one whom men could see—in order that the promise of forgiveness, salvation from sin, might be fulfilled. And now in order that men could have and know life, Jesus himself said, "I came that they may have life, and have it abundantly (John 10:10)."

That promise of life was fulfilled, first of all, by the example of our Lord. He was exactly what Pilate said he was, "the Man." The Roman governor testified that he found no fault with Jesus—and remember that Pilate was a reluctant witness. Try as he would he could not criticize the Lord.

What are some of the marks of this faultlessness? First, he was a man of integrity. I like that word and what it signifies. Literally, it means wholeness, not fractured. We have this same root meaning in the word integer (a whole number) and even in the word integrate, where all the parts are united into one whole. So it is in this word integrity. The same clear through. Not a show on the outside and rotten in the heart, but, like sterling silver clear through; or like solid gold, not plate, with some baser metal within. The same stance on every day, whether that stance is politic or not. He did not say one thing one day and another on another day. He did not stand on one set of principles today and reverse himself tomorrow. He had integrity—wholeness.

I want to emphasize that though I have outlined this in only a few words, it is of no less importance than some of the other points I shall make at greater length. The fact is that this is the most important of all. Here is where greatness begins, has its rise. Like a spring-fed lake, the source of the cold clear water is up in the hills, far away from the contamination of the city. Jesus was great, he brought the hope of life to men because like his Father he was a whole person. I have known a lot of people in my life, but I have known only a few of whom I could say that they were whole persons—and none of them were whole even as he was. In the measure that they were whole people, they were like unto him.

In the second place, he was extraordinarily concerned about the needs of the people whom he met, particularly about the needs of the least, the last, and the lost, and he went to all lengths to meet those needs. It made no difference in his concern whether the person was a child or a mature adult, whether he was famous or of ill repute, whether he was rich or poor, honored or despised. In fact, he seemed to bend over backwards to be of assistance to those who had little and deserved less, by all the standards by which men make judgment. He seemed to understand that their needs were even greater than those of other people. And when men were particularly kind to him or tried to win his favor or plaudits, he brought them back again to the fundamental issue: "As you did it to one of the least of these my brethren, you did it to me." His was never a favor that was patronizing or disparaging. Actually, his help was the kind that causes a man to lift up his head, stiffen his backbone, and walk away more the man than before. He never impoverished a soul.

This all has two applications to our living. First, he set a model for us to follow in being concerned about our fellowmen and their needs. And this is not easy for any of us. Our own needs, our desires are so much closer to us, and more real, and seem more insistent than the needs and desires of our brothers. We tend to be more concerned with our itching than we are with the retching of our brother in his unfilled hunger. Unless we do some very basic compensating, we shall never be able to strike the right balance between our needs and the needs of our fellows. Our needs will always seem so much more important to us.

Not with Jesus. He set the pattern plainly before us. Unless a man is willing to deny himself—deny himself, not deny himself of something, but deny *himself*—he cannot follow me. "You shall love your neighbor as yourself." Nothing in that law to the effect that one cannot think highly of self. In fact, just the opposite. But you have to balance over against that as great concern, interest, and love for neighbor as for self. The best I ever heard this expressed was by the great English layman C. S. Lewis, in his book *Screwtape Letters.* I am not sure you are acquainted with this unique piece of writing. The book is made up of letters which the head devil, Screwtape, is writing to his nephew, Wormwood, who has been sent to bedevil a man; Screwtape is trying to coach the younger devil. He is writing in this letter about humility.

By this method thousands of humans have been brought to think humility means pretty women trying to believe they are ugly and clever men trying to believe that they are fools. . . . The enemy [God] wants to bring the man to a state of mind in which he could design the best cathedral in the world, and know it to be the best, and rejoice in the fact without being any more (or less) or otherwise glad at having done it than he would be if it had been done by another.*

---

* C. S. Lewis, *Screwtape Letters* (New York: Macmillan, 1943), p. 73. Used by permission.

Isn't that wonderful? Not despising of self, but loving one's neighbor as oneself—as much, as fully, as respectfully as oneself. To do this we must be able to imagine ourself in the shoes of our neighbor and understand how life must look to him.

The second question which all this poses is the question concerning the essence of love. If we are to love, what does this entail? This is a point which is very important. It does not consist in automatically and unthinkingly doing the things which Jesus did. It is not that easy. It consists, rather, in having the kind of a spirit, mind, heart that Jesus had, and when that is achieved, then the acts stemming from that spirit will take care of themselves. This is easy for us to see in other people, but not so easy for us to understand in ourselves. We seem always to be looking for a set of blueprints, a bill of particulars, some easy-to-apply directions that will lead us into the way of love. You might as well quit looking, for they are not to be found; and if they were, they would not work or suffice. Perhaps the best illustration of this point is that of a mother of two different children, or two different mothers of two different children. Even Dr. Spock could not write a book telling each mother exactly what she ought to do at exactly what time in order to express her love for her child. She has to use her imagination, her head, in order to know what the child needs at each particular time, and how differently each individual child must be treated.

Now, do not misunderstand me. Information is important. If a mother does not know the difference between a food and a drug and uses them without discrimination, her child will die. But this does not mean that if she has all the information in the world, but does not use her head and heart as to the way to apply this information, her child will be strong. That is, between the two, love is much more an attitude, a feeling, a matter of the heart than it is a matter of information. So we need to look to our attitudes, if we are to be like our Lord. If the attitude is right, the deeds will take care of themselves. If the deeds are right but the attitude is wrong, the situation will not be saved by slavishly following the pattern of our Lord's life. In one of the epistles of Paul, if you will allow me a very free translation (actually it is an interpretation more than a translation) he said, "If your heart is right then you can do as you please—for you are sure to please the right." Now, again I warn you that right intentions cannot take the place of accurate information—but the intention is the more important of the two. Love is a spirit, not a set of instructions or slavishly following them as if they had been learned by rote.

All this does not mean that we have not received some guidelines from him. He says that we must be forgiving. In fact, he says that God forgives us (and all of us must have God's forgiveness) in the measure of our forgiveness of others. If we apply that standard, how much forgiveness can we expect from God?

Forgive us our debts (trespasses, sins),
    As we also have forgiven our debtors; . . .
For if you forgive men their trespasses, your heavenly Father also will forgive you; but if you do not forgive men their trespasses, neither will your Father forgive your trespasses.

—Matthew 6:12, 14-15

Or there is the matter that love can brook no delay, no excuses. Jesus tells the story of the man who gave a great banquet. According to the custom of the day he had sent out invitations and the guests had accepted. Then, according to the further custom, when the banquet was ready to be served, he sent his servants to summon his guests. But they all began to make excuses. One said that

40

he had bought a field and had to go inspect it; and another, that he had bought five yoke of oxen and had to test them; and another, that he had married a wife and therefore could not come. And when this report was brought back to the lord, he said, "None of those men who were invited shall taste my banquet."

Or again he told about the Pharisees who were so meticulous about the outside of the cup, but never washed the inside. Or about them that tithe down to the last mint leaf in their garden but do not care at all about the weightier matters of the law—righteousness and peace and joy. "You blind Pharisee! first cleanse the inside of the cup and of the plate, that the outside also may be clean (Matt. 23:26)." Religion, Christianity, our faith is a spirit, it is not slavishly keeping to a set of directions. And if the spirit is wrong, the deeds can never be right. Certainly I do not need to labor this point any longer. Again, the best illustration is in our home life. One can begin married life with a perfect set of rules which set forth when and how each deed is to be done—but if love is not there, it will be like a sounding brass and a tinkling cymbal. The attitude is the important ingredient in the good life.

PART II
STORIES JESUS TOLD

CHAPTER 4
THE
LOST
SON

In the first three chapters we have been considering how God broke into our life at Christmas, in order that we could not only have the experience of hearing about him and his relationship to men, but that supremely we might have the opportunity to see what God would be like if he were a man. It is so much easier to understand by observing than by reading about that which we observe. The text, you remember, was from the prologue to the Gospel of John (1:14): "And the Word" (this that had been written in history, sung about in psalms, spoken orally—this that was contained in words) "became flesh and dwelt among us, full of grace and truth; we have beheld his glory, glory as of the only Son from the Father."

Now, as an instrument of teaching, second only to seeing the likeness of God in a man, is becoming acquainted with some of the stories which Jesus told; for the stories he told were always related for a purpose, as windows through which one could observe the truth. These stories which Jesus told are called parables. A parable is a story which teaches a truth. As a boy I learned that a parable was an earthly story with a heavenly meaning. Well, that is a good definition if you do not put too much stress on the "heavenly meaning" part. For the glimpses of truth which we see in these parables are really in order that truth can be applied to the way we live in the here and now. With this background let us look at a few of the stories Jesus told.

45

We need, however, to get one idea firmly implanted in our mind. A parable has only one meaning, one lesson to teach. Great violence has been done to these parables by trying to make every detail teach a different truth. George Henry Hubbard, in a book now over fifty years old, says, "The typical parable of Jesus is the embodiment of one central thought to which all details are subordinate." In an article in the *Interpreter's Bible*, Walter Russell Bowie writes:

> In Augustine's [who lived in the sixth century] treatment the swift parable of Jesus [the good Samaritan] is turned into an amazing allegory. The "certain man" who went down from Jerusalem to Jericho is Adam. Jerusalem is the city of Peace from which Adam fell. Jericho is our human mortality toward which he goes. The flesh and blood thieves of the parable who fall upon the real man on the Jericho road become now the devil and his angels, who strip Adam of his immortality, . . . and leave him stripped of his communion with God. . . . The priest and Levite represent the priesthood and ministry of the Old Testament from which Adam could expect nothing. The Samaritan is Christ himself. The binding up of the wounds is restraint of sin, oil is the comfort of the hope.*

The beast on which the wounded man was placed was the Incarnation, and the ride to the Inn was the way a man is saved by faith in the "Incarnation." Do not you see that the whole thing becomes a bit ridiculous? In these parables Jesus wanted to make a point, to illustrate a truth, and so he told a story, much in the same way we

---

* Walter Russell Bowie, "The Parables," *The Interpreter's Bible* (Nashville: Abingdon Press, 1951), VII, 173-74. Used by permission.

would tell a story. Every detail was not apropos to the development of the plot—just the main point.

Now to the parable of the prodigal son. That parable is a story which Jesus told to illustrate, to reveal, the forgiving love of God.

We begin with a young lad who wants to use his own mind and make his own decisions. That is natural enough. So one day the boy asks for his share of the inheritance that someday would come to him. Why his father consented to give it to him before he was mature enough to handle it correctly is a mystery, but not one of the main points of the parable. The boy does get his inheritance and goes away from home. If that were not true, there would be no point to the story. Away from home, the lad is also away from all the restrictions imposed upon him by his father. He is now free—or is he? Perhaps there is never anyone who is so little free as those who think they have thrown off the old restraints. That has been written into the history of this age, as well as the age out of which this parable came. As youngsters, we know so much better than all of the traditions which have strait-jacketed our elders. Now, do not misunderstand me. Just because a thing is old is no reason why it is perfect, anymore than just because it is new makes it either worthless or of value. Something is of worth because it is of worth, not because it is either old or new.

At any rate, this lad was willing to throw overboard everything that had been practiced through long years. He was going out on his own. In a way, this is what we must all do; go out on our own. No parent worthy of the name would want his child to be tied to him all his life. The greatest compliment that children can pay their parents is to become independent—but that does not mean playing fast and loose with all the principles for which the family stands.

In the far country to which the boy traveled he lived a long way from his parents not only in distance, but also in goals and habits of life. It was indeed a "far country" from the way in which the boy had been reared. It ended the way so many such experiences end, in disaster. As long as the money held out, the lad was the center of attention; he had many so-called friends—but the moment he had spent all his inheritance, then he was friendless. I suppose it is too much to expect a young person on his first adventure to understand that this will be the case. But it has been written in the history of the world time and time again. It ought not to be necessary for every lad and lass to learn the hard way the lessons written in history. There ought to be a better and more certain method of transferring the know-how of one generation to the next. But the boy learned only by the more difficult way.

Hungry, disillusioned, despondent, discouraged, the boy took a job feeding swine. I do not want to fall prey to the charge against which I have warned you—trying to find a meaning in every detail—but here is certainly a meaning. You know that pork was forbidden to Jews, and for this boy, reared in the strictest manner of his people, to be reduced to the job of feeding pigs was indeed a bitter experience. But then too, it gave him a lot of time to do some deep thinking. And what a blessing that was! He needed a chance to rethink his values, to relearn what was the highest good, the goal of a man's life.

Luke, who records the parable (15:11-32) has the Master using a wonderful touch. The story says, "when he came to himself." It is interesting to note, and encouraging, that though the principles in which we are reared may seem to be covered up by a thousand accretions of life, they usually are there, and sometime, even in unexpected ways, places, and times, they will crop up. "When he came to himself," the real boy, and the things for which he really stood, came to the fore. I like that touch.

And he said, "How many of my father's hired servants have bread enough and to spare, but I perish here with hunger!" (Perhaps that last phrase, "perish with hunger," was a little bit of self-pity.) At least he was seeing for the first time how deep was his need, what a mistake he had made. And so he said to himself, "I will arise and go to my father, and I will say to him, 'Father, I have sinned against heaven and before you; I am no longer worthy to be called your son; treat me as one of your hired servants.' " Certainly it took no little swallowing of pride to bring himself to such a decision and such an act. But costly to pride though it was, he began that journey.

And now to the father, who is the center and the hero of the story. The story goes on: "But while he was yet at a distance, his father saw him and had compassion." Did you ever stop to ask yourself why it was that the father saw him even though the boy was at a great distance? It has always seemed to me it must have been that the father had spent a good deal of time looking down that long road, hoping against hope that someday it would happen just as it was happening: the boy would come home. Otherwise, he never would have seen him until he actually had arrived and knocked. But not this father. The father saw him even when the boy was a long distance away. And then what did the father do? Say to himself, I will wait until he makes the first move; I will let him eat his humble pie; I will not make it easier for him; he must confess his mistakes? Hardly. It was an altogether different spirit which was actuating that father—for more than anything else he wanted the boy home, not home so much in the sense of being within the house in which his father lived, but rather at one with the truth upon which that home had been built. And so the father ran and threw his arms about him and fell on his neck and kissed him. And when the boy began the speech which he had rehearsed, I think the father must have clapped his hand over the boy's mouth so the words could not come out. The father had no joy in seeing the humiliation of the lad. He wanted to make it as easy as possible for the boy to come home. And so he cried out, "Bring quickly the best robe, and put it on him; and put a ring on his hand, and shoes on his feet; and bring the fatted calf and kill it, and let us eat and make merry; for this my son was dead, and is alive again; he was lost, and is found."

I want to particularly call your attention to the little word quickly in the text. One of my preacher friends had advertised on his bulletin board that on the next Sunday he would preach on the theme "God's in a Hurry." Another of my friends saw John during the week and said, "What under the sun are you going to say about 'God's in a Hurry' and what will be your text? We usually talk about the fact that God has a lot of time. A thousand years are but as a day, and day is a thousand years. We say the mills of the gods grind slowly though they do grind exceedingly fine. We talk about the patience of God, seldom about his impatience." "Ah," said my friend, "didn't you ever notice that little word quickly in the parable of the prodigal son?" "Bring quickly." God's in a hurry to save his people. Isn't that a fine touch? "Bring quickly."

A couple of things need to be pointed out. The father was eager to receive the boy, to grant him forgiveness, and to make him again a son. Such is the way of real fathers worthy of the name. The father in the parable—and he represents God—was and is and always shall be forgiving; not requiring his pound of flesh or the humiliation of the boy; glad to have him back; making it easy for the boy to come back. This is one of the very pointed teachings of the scripture. "But the steadfast love of the Lord is from everlasting to everlasting." If you want to see just how this works you can do no better than to read the prophecy of Hosea. This is a remarkable story and points out how Hosea learned, in the hard school of his own forgiveness, how merciful God is. Do you recall the story? Hosea had a wife whom he loved dearly—but (to put it in modern parlance) she ran off with another man. When this second man tired of his new mistress, he sold her into slavery. Now, one would have thought that Hosea would

50

have had enough of this woman—but no. He hears of her plight as a slave, and so he goes and buys her back and makes her his wife again. And then all of a sudden it comes to him that if he could be so forgiving, how much more will God forgive those whom he loves. You ought to read that story—it stretches your mind so that you can understand the ways of the Lord.

If you will allow me to say it, in human literature the father in the parable represents God, and he never shows up better than he does in the parable of the lost son. In that story you begin to know what it is that the Word is talking about when it says, "As a father pities his children, so the Lord pities those who fear him (Ps. 103:13)" (even when they are disobedient).

Then we have the postlude to this story—the incident of the elder son. I am not going to say too much about that, else it will blot out for you the forgiveness of the father. Suffice it to say that the elder son was just as untrue, in an altogether different way, to the father's spirit and the father's heart as was the young boy. He too played fast and loose with all for which the father stood—love, patience, forgiveness, compassion. And there is this that needs to be added. When a man indulges in the evil deeds of the younger boy, there is more chance that he will see and understand his sins than if he harbors the resentful attitude of the older boy. It is very hard for us to see in ourselves the tragedy of small-heartedness, of pettiness, of selfishness.

The older boy was quick to judge the younger as having spent his inheritance on wild women and song—but he never once thought that he too had betrayed all for which the father stood and that the father was as much a heartbroken man from the spirit of the older boy as from the profligate deeds of the younger one. Both boys were a disappointment to the father. Can you not hear the disillusionment in the words, "Son, you are always with me, and all that is mine is yours. It was fitting to make merry and be glad, for this your brother was dead, and is alive;

he was lost, and is found." I think part of the sorrow in the voice of the father is due to the fact that he really did not believe, because of the petty spirit that possessed the boy's heart, that the elder son would understand even in a small measure what he (the father) was talking about. For me, and I may judge the older boy too harshly, I cannot see the turn of hand's difference in the measure of their betrayal of the father and all for which he stood. The point is that God was willing to forgive them both.

What a God we have, so willing, so eager to receive us again as his children! I think I began to understand this a little more when one day I ran upon some lines of free verse, which set it forth so plainly.

> If I were God
> And man made a mire
> Of things: war, hatred,
> Murder, lust, cob-webs
> Of infamy, entangling
> The heart and soul—
> I would sweep him
> To one side and start anew.
> (I think I would.)
> If I did this,
> Would I be God?*

"But the steadfast love of the Lord is from everlasting to everlasting (Ps. 103:17)." "For God so loved the world." "In this is love, not that we loved God but that he loved us and sent his Son to be the expiation for our sins."

How better can we learn this than by hearing again the words, "There was a man who had two sons. . . . 'Bring quickly the best robe . . . for this my son was dead, and is alive again; he was lost, and is found.' " God's in a hurry to save his people.

---

* Carl S. Weist, "If I Were God." Copyright 1930, Christian Century Foundation. Reprinted by permission from the December 17, 1930 issue of *The Christian Century*.

CHAPTER 5
THE
LOST
SHEEP

We are trying to learn something about God and about life by examining some of the stories that Jesus told. Second only to learning about God by seeing him in Jesus, we learn about God and about life by looking at the stories which Jesus told. And remember, each of these stories really had only one point.

The story of the lost sheep now commands our attention. This, like the story of the lost son, is one of a trilogy which Jesus told to help men know about the forgiveness of God. While the order of these stories in the fifteenth chapter of Luke puts the story of the lost son after the story of the lost sheep, I am not too sure that he told them in that order. You always have to remember that the Gospel according to Luke was not written until thirty or forty years after the ministry of our Lord, and it would have been very easy for Luke not to recall the exact order. Besides that, Luke was not a disciple at the time of Jesus' ministry, and it is very unlikely that he was present. The point is that logically the parable of the lost son ought to have preceded the parable of the lost sheep—for in the latter the forgiveness of God is taken one step further than in the lost son. Here the shepherd (and the shepherd is God) does not stay at home and wait until the lost sheep returns, but he goes out seeking the lost sheep. That is a logical next step to the story of the prodigal.

But more of that later. Perhaps we ought to read the parable first to see exactly what it says.

> What man of you, having a hundred sheep, if he has lost one of them, does not leave the ninety-nine in the wilderness, and go after the one which is lost, until he finds it? And when he has found it, he lays it on his shoulders, rejoicing. And when he comes home, he calls together his friends and his neighbors, saying to them, "Rejoice with me, for I have found my sheep which was lost." Even so, I tell you, there will be more joy in heaven over one sinner who repents than over ninety-nine righteous persons who need no repentance.
>
> —Luke 15:4-7

The sheep was lost. How? Well, there are a dozen possible ways, but there is one which has always made sense to me, because it is the way so many of us become lost. A farmer was talking to the city man, and the latter said, "How does a sheep get lost?" And the answer came back immediately, "They just nibble themselves lost. They keep their heads down, wander from one green tuft to another, come to a hole in the fence—and they never seem to be able to find the hole by which they could get back again."

That is about the way it is with us. We never intend to get lost (some folks may, but not most of us). But little by little we slip into ways that separate us from God. We nibble ourselves lost. We never intend to quit going to church, we just stay away one Sunday, and that makes it easier to stay away the second Sunday, and soon we are not going at all, and we never seem to notice it or have any pangs of conscience. We never intend to live a self-centered life—but self-centeredness is usually the result, not of a conscious decision, but of a series of small choices that because of their number become habitual. We never intend to live a life of "passing by on the other side," but the first time we do such a thing, there is such a good reason (or excuse)—as if there is ever a reason for not being our brother's brother. We just slip into habits which we did not intend, but that does not make us any the less lost. The sheep in the story was as lost when he simply nibbled himself astray as if, by conscious choice, he had decided to leave the flock. This part of the parable is a chapter out of the living of far too many of us.

The second important facet of this story is that sheep that is lost is only one percent of the flock. I can almost hear you say (if we can think ourselves into the role of the shepherd), "We have responsibility not only for the one but ninety-nine times as much responsibility for the ninety-nine; and therefore we had better choose the greater responsibility and let the lesser one go." Maybe by this time it has been set upon by wild beasts or fallen into a stream and drowned. Maybe we would not be able to find it anyway; and all the time we were searching, the ninety-nine would be left without attention. We get very practical when we face a decision like this, and practicality is all on the side of the ninety-nine. But not with the forgiving God. He leaves the ninety-nine in the sheepfold, at no small risk to his flock and to his reputation as a shepherd, and he goes out to look for the lost sheep. The relation between the one sheep and this shepherd—this forgiving God of ours—is a one-to-one relationship. That takes priority over the relationship to the flock.

Now, this is not a new concept in the New Testament. Always in the Old Testament, God is described as the God of Abraham, Isaac, and Jacob, and of every individual man, woman, and child. In the Gospel of John (in that very precious chapter where Jesus describes himself as the Good Shepherd), it is recorded that "the sheep hear his voice, and he calls his own sheep by name and leads them out (10:3)." One of the most startling truths recorded in the Book, but confirmed by our hearts, is that no one of us is lost in the whole of mankind. We are all persons, individual persons to God, and he cannot be content until he goes out seeking each individual soul. The God of Abraham and Isaac and Jacob and Mary and Sue and John and Henry and Ben. The ninety-nine were not enough and never could be enough, when one was missing.

So in large letters it ought to be written on our hearts, so that we never can overlook it or forget it: "What man of you, having a hundred sheep, if he has lost one of them, does not leave the ninety-nine in the wilderness, and go after the one which is lost, until he finds it?" You and I amidst all the mass of mankind—three billions of us and by the end of the century six billions—you and I are precious to God, so precious that when we have need, when because of our stubbornness we shut him out, he will not let us go. He comes seeking us. What a loving God we have! If I were God, I do not think I could be that forgiving. I say again, what a great God we have!

This sentence is followed with another clause. He goes after the one which is lost "until he finds it." Perhaps this is the best touch of the whole story. There is no place that God will not go, nothing that he will not do in order to lead his children back to the fold. "Until he finds it." Whenever I think of this phrase I think of the way most children look for their lost possessions. If with one quick sweep of the eyes it is not discovered in plain sight, they usually cry to their mother, "I can't find it." What is recorded in the fifteenth chapter of Luke is not that kind of hunting. He looks until he finds it.

One of my very favorite pictures is one which many years ago came to me as a gift. It is by the well-known artist Soord. It is about this parable and is the artist's effort to make the parable, and the love and compassion of the shepherd, plain. Soord makes this part, "until he finds it," evident by placing the time of the finding just at the moment when the sun is coming up over the eastern horizon. The shepherd had searched all night until he found the sheep, and he would have searched longer if it had been necessary. "Until he finds it." I am so glad that Jesus included those words in this story. Albert Edward Bailey, in his classic *The Gospel in Art,* has this to say about this painting:

> The trouble with most "Good Shepherds" is that they are good for nothing. The theme has been handled over and over again from the time of the Catacombs down, but usually one sees the same type of picture, the figure of a pretty man holding a lamb in his bosom. To one who has seen shepherds in Palestine there is something particularly repugnant in such a representation. No real shepherd ever wore the elegant draperies that adorn artists' models. No shepherd ever sported such ambrosial curls or posed so gracefully, or showed such absence of character in his face. On the contrary, when you come upon a real shepherd in the shepherd's country, something is apt to grip your heart and your throat. Shepherding there is a man's job! There you see the rough jacket made of a fleece turned wool-side in; the bare bronzed bosom, the bare legs scratched with the thorns, the rough shoes of rawhide, the great club of oak with its knot on the end heavy enough to fell a bear; the high-stepping stride and the muscles like steel that endure the tramps over rocky country, the fearless eye that can face danger alone; and you often see a lamb in the strong arms. Such is the person Jesus had in mind when he said "I am the Good Shepherd."
>
> Soord has presented something like the original parable. . . . The sheep is lost. No careful shepherd

would have led his flock into such a pasture as this; the foolish sheep herself is responsible for the situation. Too much self-confidence, too adventurous a spirit, ignorance of the precipices and of the eagles circling high in the blue and waiting for things to die.*

And now the sheep is found.

But there is still another facet to this story. And when he finds it, he lays it on his shoulders rejoicing. And when he comes home he calls his friends and neighbors, saying to them, " 'Rejoice with me, for I have found my sheep which was lost.' Even so, I tell you, there will be more joy in heaven over one sinner who repents than over ninety-nine righteous persons who need no repentance." I have only one question to ask about that last sentence. Who of us belongs to the ninety-nine who need no repentance? The parable is about joy: the joy of finding, the joy of restoring, the joy of forgiving. The parable is about joy. The joy of finding and the joy of the kingdom.

Now, I am going to be very pointed. Most of us do not know much about the joy of finding, for most of us do not do much hunting. I am appalled at the lethargy, at the disinterest of most of our churches in this matter of going out to win people back into the kingdom, people who have nibbled themselves lost. I am not talking only about the United Church of Christ. I am talking about most of our middle-class, middle-of-the-road Protestant churches. Either we have something to share with people —a gospel to proclaim, a faith to which we ought to give witness—or we do not. If we do not have anything worth sharing, then it is perfectly all right for us to seal our lips. But if we have something, if we know what it is to be found, then God forgive us, why do we not do something

---

* Albert Edward Bailey, *The Gospel in Art* (Boston: The Pilgrim Press, 1944) , pp. 174-75.

about it? The world needs to hear about the gospel. Without that message the world and the people in it are lost. The business of the church, as I see it, the primary business of the church is to go forth to witness, to witness to society and to witness to individuals. And somehow we are not doing that as we should. Some of us do not even see the importance of this. Others think it can be delayed for more important matters. But there are no more important matters.

"What man of you, having a hundred sheep, if he has lost one of them, does not leave the ninety-nine in the wilderness, and go after the one which is lost, until he finds it?"

In one of the old gospel hymns, which a few of you may remember, this message is expressed so very well. I give it to you.

There were ninety and nine that safely lay
In the shelter of the fold,
But one was out on the hills away,
Far from the gates of gold—
Away on the mountains wild and bare,
Away from the tender Shepherd's care,
Away from the tender Shepherd's care.

"Lord, Thou hast here Thy ninety and nine;
Are they not enough for Thee?"
But the Shepherd made answer:
"This of mine has wandered away from me;
And, although the road be rough and steep,
I go to the desert to find my sheep,
I go to the desert to find my sheep."

But none of the ransomed ever knew
How deep were the waters cross'd;
Nor how dark was the night that the Lord pass'd thro'
Ere He found His sheep that was lost.

Out in the desert He heard its cry—
Sick and helpless and ready to die,
Sick and helpless and ready to die.

"Lord, whence are those blood-drops all the way
That mark out the mountain's track?"
"They were shed for one who had gone astray
Ere the Shepherd could bring him back."
"Lord, whence are Thy hands so rent and torn?"
"They were pierc'd tonight by many a thorn.
They were pierc'd tonight by many a thorn."

But all thro' the mountains, thunder-riven,
And up from the rocky steep,
There rose a glad cry to the gate of heaven,
"Rejoice! I have found my sheep!"
And the angels echoed around the throne,
"Rejoice, for the Lord brings back His own!
Rejoice, for the Lord brings back His own!"

CHAPTER 6
THE
LEAVEN

Now we study the parable of the leaven. This is considered for at least two reasons: first, because it has been so terribly abused by that group of interpreters who want to make every detail have some meaning; and second, because in this period of time, when there is so much that is discouraging, it seems we need the encouragement of this story that fell from the lips of our Lord. The parable consists in just one sentence, or, as we say in the Bible texts, one verse. I am going to use the wording from *The New English Bible* (by the way, the parable is found both in Matthew and Luke) : "The kingdom of God, what shall I compare it with? It is like yeast which a woman took and mixed with half a hundredweight of flour till it was all leavened (Luke 13:20-21)." There is no single verse of scripture which is more encouraging to me, in these days when evil seems so strong and seems to flourish so unhampered, than this one.

First, on the negative side: you remember I said a moment ago that one of the reasons why I chose to talk about this parable is because it has been misinterpreted so often. In the whole Hebrew literature, leaven—yeast—always stood for evil. That was the reason why at the time of the Passover the whole house had to be cleaned and any yeast had to be thrown out. And of course I need hardly remind you that yeast did not in those days come in small squares as it does today, but was saved in liquid form from one baking to the next. When I was a boy at home and my mother baked bread, she still followed this old custom. Sometimes she and a neighbor woman used this pint of what she called "starter" together, for the more it was used, the better.

In the Hebrew mind, therefore, leaven—yeast—stood for something evil, not good, contaminating. So you have a whole school of exegetes, biblical interpreters, who are dead sure that this was what Jesus was talking about. Then where it is said in the King James Version that the women hid the leaven in three measures, these same men try to find some meaning in that. For instance, they say it means the three great powers of that day: Rome, Egypt, and Assyria. Or they say it means body, mind, and spirit. You already know along with most biblical scholars, I am sure, that these parables have but one meaning—and that when you try to get a lot of symbolism out of them, you do them violence. Jesus was here trying to show his followers how the kingdom grew, developed, expanded—and that is it. The kingdom was not evil, and he did not have in mind just three dimensions of it. Let us allow it to speak to us.

There are five points which need to be presented. First, it does not take much yeast to make a difference. The woman took a "little" leaven. Now, this does not indicate that we should devote only a little of our time, our talent, and our money to the kingdom—not that. But it does mean that we do not have to be discouraged because we are able to do so little relative to the colossal dimensions of the problems. Somehow this is one of our great "hangups" today. The problems which we face as people and a nation are so great and complex, that it is easy for us to get the idea that what little we can do will have no effect at all. How wrong we are! One only has to read biography and history to know that all the great movements in history were started by one person getting an idea and turning that idea loose in the world. Who was it that said,

"There is nothing so strong as an idea whose time has come"? You may not be able to do great things, but the small things which you can do, if you do them, may move the world greatly. I know of no idea which needs more to be spoken of than this idea: "a little leaven."

I had to settle this in my own mind and life once and for all. As a young man I had visions and hopes of being able to preach like Harry Emerson Fosdick. But it was not long before I came to the sad realization that I was not going to arrive at that place in life; that I really was not called of God to be a second Fosdick; that what I was called to do, what God expected me to do, was to preach the word in the best way I could. And so I settled for that. I am just a one-talented person, like most of you; but God does expect me to use that one talent for his will and for my fellowmen. What I can do does not seem much, but I am determined I will do that. The woman does not put a hundredweight of yeast into a little bit of flour. It is the other way around. The yeast is small in proportion to the meal, but it has to be put in there.

That brings us then to the second thing which needs to be stressed: the leaven is let loose in the meal, as the word of God has to be let loose in the world. As long as the leaven is in the jar, nothing happens; the liquid was saturated with the yeast plants and that was as much as could get in there. But the minute the yeast was mixed with the flour, then something began to happen. This is what the parable of the leaven emphasizes—the necessity for you, as a people, to be willing to hide the leaven of your faith in your community. If you keep it in the four walls of a church, nothing will happen—except the tragedy that perhaps you will lose even the faith you have. You know, there is a strange mathematics about our faith: the more we give it away, the more we have; and the more we hoard it, the less we have. That does not make sense mathematically, but faith runs by a different mathematics.

The woman hid the little bit of yeast she had in a lot of meal. Now, the strange thing about this process is that after she hid it there, the dough did not look much different from the way it did before. This confuses some of us no end. If we could go out and make a big change in our community in a day or two, I am sure we would be more eager to go out; but it does not work that way, and the kingdom does not grow that way. You mix, hide, the yeast in the flour so you can see the yeast no longer, so you no longer have it. You give it up. If you go to some words of our Lord they may point the way: "Unless a grain of wheat falls into the earth and dies, it remains alone; but if it dies, it bears much fruit (John 12:24)." You have to bury the yeast—give it up—and what you have then looks as it did before. But it begins to work, quietly and relentlessly. This is really the main impact of this parable. Quietly and relentlessly.

We humans are not so sure of this. We think that unless some great noise is made, some great catastrophic change takes place, as in the twinkling of an eye, nothing is happening. I find this true about the relationship between some of our pastors and their congregations. These pastors are not "the spellbinding kind" and yet solidly and quietly they build. And the tragedy is that many times they leave for another field before the worth of their ministry is understood or realized. Then it is too late. The yeast grows quietly, and so slowly that just a glance will not reveal to you that it is growing at all. But never be misled. Quietly, relentlessly—no way to shut it off except by baking it and killing the yeast. All of you have seen dough rise to the top of a crock or mixing bowl, and overflow it. Who would have thought that would happen when you began—except that you had learned by experience. Well, that is the hope and vision for your church. Put the leaven into this community, and it will overflow the crock which is your church. But you have to let it loose. You do not put the leaven of the gospel in the meal with a shotgun at a long distance. You go out into the world, out into the homes, out into the marketplace and hide it there, mix it in there—and then give it a little time to grow. It will grow, never fear for that. It will grow relentlessly. But it must be mixed in.

The next thing is that we are not responsible for the results. We are only responsible for the hiding, the planting, the mixing. This is made so very plain in the prophecy of Isaiah:

> For as the rain and the snow come down from heaven,
>   and return not thither but water the earth,
> making it bring forth and sprout,
>   giving seed to the sower and bread to the eater,
> so shall my word be that goes forth from my mouth;
>   it shall not return to me empty,
> but it shall accomplish that which I purpose,
>   and prosper in the thing for which I sent it.
>   —Isaiah 55:10-11

I must tell you that as a Christian this has always been a great comfort to me. I really am not responsible, God does not hold me accountable, for what happens after I preach or live out the gospel among a people. He only holds me accountable for the fact that my words and my living must exemplify the Christ and the forgiving God who sent him and sent me. If that were not true I do not believe that I could have stood up against the task all these years. And so it seems to me that this ought to be a great comfort to you. Your part of this task is clear—or is it? That is what I am concerned about—that you understand that you are to sow the seed, you are to hide the yeast in the world, in your neighborhood, so the word is to go out through your mouth and your life; and then you can leave the rest to God. Did you ever hear the story about the lifeguards who saw a ship in distress at a time when the waves were running as high as a house? One of them resisted going to the rescue, saying no one could come back in a sea like that. And the captain quietly but dramatically said, "We don't have to come back, but we've got to go out." I tell you this is the task that you are up against in this church. Going out. Hiding the yeast, proclaiming the word. Then God will take care of the result.

And that brings us to the last, and in a way the greatest, truth in this story. When the leaven is mixed with the meal and you give it a little time, the whole lump is leavened. The whole lot of it. This is what I must keep on telling myself—for there are so many indications these days that this is not likely to happen. I say to you frankly, the church is having a harder time these days than at any other time I can remember, almost a harder time than I can read about in history. Ministers are hard pressed to keep up their courage. Laymen and laywomen face opposition and ridicule of which I never would have dreamed two decades ago. We had a rather easy time then, compared to these days—though it has never been easy to be a Christian, a witnessing living Christian.

Well, in these days when the outlook is not too rosy, when so many problems confront us, when the way is hard and the going is rough, never lose sight of the fact that God has set forth what will be the end of it all (if we are faithful, if we are faithful): the leavening of the whole lump, the kingdom. And that is what we want, isn't it? The kingdom, the rule of God in the hearts and ways of men? That is what the kingdom means. Jesus is saying that this is going to come, not spectacularly, with a lot of noise, but slowly and surely like the growth of yeast, until there is not one particle of the flour that has not been permeated and changed. But it depends upon our faithfulness in making the word known, by our lips and by our lives.

CHAPTER 7
THE
TEN
VIRGINS

Again, many of us are inclined to procrastinate in readying ourselves for the forgiveness of God, and so to make it crystal clear that God does not countenance procrastination, Jesus told the story of the ten virgins. It is found in Matthew 25:1-13.

Then the kingdom of heaven shall be compared to ten maidens who took their lamps and went to meet the bridegroom. Five of them were foolish, and five were wise. For when the foolish took their lamps, they took no oil with them; but the wise took flasks of oil with their lamps. As the bridegroom was delayed, they all slumbered and slept. But at midnight there was a cry, "Behold, the bridegroom! Come out to meet him." Then all those maidens rose and trimmed their lamps. And the foolish said to the wise, "Give us some of your oil, for our lamps are going out." But the wise replied, "Perhaps there will not be enough for us and for you; go rather to the dealers and buy for yourselves." And while they went to buy, the bridegroom came, and those who were ready went in with him to the marriage feast; and the door was shut. Afterward the other maidens came also, saying, "Lord, lord, open to us." But he replied, "Truly, I say to you, I do not know you." Watch, therefore, for you know neither the day nor the hour.

This presumption upon the forgiveness and mercy of God is a long-standing one. Men have been so presuming since the beginning of time. There is always tomorrow; never do today what you can put off until tomorrow. There is plenty of time. But the truth is that even with God there is not plenty of time. He wants his children with him in his heart and in his home. He does not want to wait until the last minute. He says to us and to all, "Watch, therefore, for you know neither the day nor the hour."

Life has a way, like sand, of running through our fingers. We cannot stay this aging process. Our life looks long when we look ahead, but when most of our earthly days have been lived, it looks very short as we look back. We do not have forever to turn to God. I take it that there are three applications of this parable. For the early church there is no question about the fact that they were looking for an early return of our Lord and the establishment of his kingdom, and so the teaching was that everybody ought to be ready for that second Advent. Now twenty centuries have come and gone and he has not yet returned in the flesh, so to many of us this application is not as pressing as it was to those people of the early church. There are those who are not really sure that the second Advent will come at a certain point of time, but they believe that Christ is always coming to men. Whichever school of thought you follow, the truth is that no man ought to presume on the amount of time which he has been allotted or the amount of time from the first Advent to the second. This is one of the applications of the story, and though to many people that coming does not seem imminent, it is a factor with which we ought to come to terms.

The second aspect of it is the matter of our own death. Nobody knows how many days we have ahead of us, months, or years. Of this thing we are sure, however:

that there will come an end to earthly life and that we, like our fathers, will be gathered by "the great reaper." Many men put off turning to God in quest of forgiveness and salvation. In our day and generation, preaching does not emphasize this as much as it was emphasized in a former day; but that it is real and ought to be taken into consideration is unquestionable. As far as the Bible sets forth, there is no chance for turning to God beyond the grave. Certainly no one would want to try to limit God by our own understanding, but at least this is sure: the word does not give us any assurance that we shall have a second chance. Therefore, we ought to use the first chance while we have it. Someone has said there is in the scriptures only one example of deathbed repentance; *one* that men might never despair and *only* one that men might never presume.

The ever-present reality is that we do not want to live out our life without the assurance of salvation and the power of God within us, no matter how soon or how long delayed our own physical death may be. I think that this was expressed in the most quoted way in 1927 in Jerusalem: "Our Fathers were impressed with the horror that men should die without Christ. We share that horror. We are also impressed with the horror that men should live without Christ." To most of us in this generation this second horror is even more real than the first. A great evangelist of a past generation would take out his watch, and as the seconds ticked away he would tell how many people in those seconds died without Christ. One could do the same about living without Christ. When we recall how much our faith has meant to us, how much comfort, satisfaction, and power have come to us through our faith, it is unthinkable that anyone should shut himself away from that faith. Yet thousands of people do; yes, millions. They are all about us. They walk the streets with us, they work in the same factories, they trade at the same stores, they meet at the same clubs. I cannot help but add that we seldom say anything to them about what they are missing. We seldom witness to the worth of our Lord. Both they and we are, therefore, missing a great opportunity. These days that go by never come again. So many of us have never known the time when we did not believe in God and in his Son, Jesus Christ, we sometimes forget that there are many people who do not share the blessing that has come to us and that therefore we are under obligation to share the truth about God with them.

While God is patient, kind, long suffering, and merciful, he cannot, in a universe like ours, give us a second chance. The days that are gone are gone. "Watch therefore, for you know neither the day nor the hour. (Matt. 25:13)."

CHAPTER 8
THE
UNMERCIFUL
SERVANT

"And forgive us our debts, As we also have forgiven our debtors. . . . For if you forgive men their trespasses, your heavenly Father also will forgive you; but if you do not forgive men their trespasses, neither will your Father forgive your trespasses (Matt. 6:12, 14-15)."

Because the forgiveness of God is so full and so free, the mistake is made in almost every generation, by people who should know better, that they can presume upon that forgiveness. Such a great gift requires a great sense of responsibility.

To make this point Jesus told the parable of the unmerciful servant, which is found in Matthew 18:21-35:

Then Peter came up and said to him "Lord, how often shall my brother sin against me, and I forgive him? As many as seven times?" Jesus said to him, "I do not say to you seven times, but seventy times seven." Therefore, the kingdom of heaven may be compared to a king who wished to settle accounts with his servants. When he began the reckoning, one was brought to him who owed him ten thousand talents; and as he could not pay, his lord ordered him to be sold, with his wife and children and all that he had, and payment to be made. So the servant fell on his knees, imploring him, "Lord, have patience with me, and I will pay you everything." And out of pity for him the lord of that servant released him and forgave him the debt. But that same servant, as he went out, came upon one of his fellow servants who owed him a hundred denarii; and seizing him by the throat he said, "Pay what you owe." So his fellow servant fell down and besought him, "Have patience with me, and I will pay you." He refused and went and put him in prison till he should pay the debt. When his fellow servants saw what had taken place, they were greatly distressed, and they went and reported to their lord all that had taken place. Then his lord summoned him and said to him, "You wicked servant! I forgave you all that debt because you besought me; and should not you have had mercy on your fellow servant, as I had mercy on you?" And in anger his lord delivered him to the jailers, till he should pay all his debt. So also my heavenly Father will do to every one of you, if you do not forgive your brother from your heart.

The logic of that parable is very plain. After a man has been fully forgiven he then is under obligation to forgive his fellowmen, even as he has been forgiven. The story is so plain and is not an unlikely one. It was the time of accounting, and one of the lord's workmen was found to owe him a large sum. The law made it plain that the lord had a right to have him imprisoned until he should pay all. But because the servant pleaded so sincerely and so genuinely, the lord forgave him the whole debt and let him go free.

In view of subsequent events it is not hard to imagine the workings of that man's mind. "Well, I got out of that easily, didn't I? If it ever happens to me again I shall try the same formula, and likely I shall go scot-free a second time. That is the kind of a one God is. He is an 'easy mark' for a plea for forgiveness. Nothing untoward can happen to me as long as the Lord is forgiving."

Then the same man went out to try to collect a debt which one of his fellow servants owed him. "Pay what you owe," he said. Then his fellow servant fell down and said, "Have patience with me, and I will pay you." He refused and went and had him put in prison until he should pay all. If that thing did not happen every day we would hardly believe it! But it is a chapter out of the way we live. Too often we see little connection between our relation to God and God's relationship to us, on the one hand, and our relationship with our fellowmen, on the other. We do not seem to understand (at least we do not always practice it) that the same mercy which we receive from God and for which we pray is then required of us in our relationship with our neighbor. We forget the words, "Forgive us our debts, as we also have forgiven our debtors." Those words are a "contract," a "covenant" between God and us. He does not promise to forgive us again and again and again, unless we develop the forgiving spirit toward our neighbors. God is not an "easy mark." When we are forgiven we do not go free of responsibility. There comes upon us a great responsibility to forgive as we have been forgiven. Or to put it differently, God makes it very plain that those who are forgiven must in turn be forgiving.

Now, for people to believe that God will forgive us again and again even though we do not forgive our fellowmen is not a new phenomenon. It is an old misunderstanding which grew up in the early church from a misinterpretation of the writings of Paul. Paul put great stress on the grace of God—his willingness to forgive us. So some men decided that the more opportunity they gave God to forgive them, the happier he would be. In Systematic Theology this is called Antinomianism, from two Greek words—*anti* (against) and *nomos* (law). According to the late Joseph Haroutunian, professor of Systematic Theology at the Chicago Divinity School, in a signed article in the *Encyclopaedia Britannica,* "Antinomianism grew out of Protestant controversy on the Law and the Gospel, but it was not unknown previously. In the early church there were those who said, 'Let us sin that grace may abound.'" To put it crudely, they thought they ought to give God an opportunity to forgive them. They would sin and then sin again so that they could all the more exemplify the grace of God. It seems to me there is nothing that is further from the truth than this.

The first and primary requirement of Jesus' way of life is that we forgive our fellowmen. Not only does our relationship to our fellowmen require this, but also our relationship with God requires it. This is the way we prove that we were sincere when we said, "God be merciful to me a sinner." As God, through Christ, has forgiven us, so we have the obligation, we have the opportunity, the privilege of forgiving our fellowmen. This is an obligation, this is a prerequisite.

This tells us as much about God as it does about the man who forgives or withholds his forgiveness. God is not some kind of a doting grandfather who thinks his grandchildren can do no wrong, who has no requirements of them, who humors and pampers. He is a father who holds the child to a discipline—a discipline that is expressed in love to be sure, but a discipline nonetheless. He is one who makes his forgiveness depend upon a man's going out and forgiving his fellowmen. He is a man who lives in a relationship of forgiveness and mercy with his fellowmen.

How else would we want God to be? What a disappointment it would be to us if he were otherwise, even as sometimes we are a disappointment to our children when we do not hold them to a discipline. What if we could get away with anything in relationship to God; what if God did not require of us that we act foursquare, that we be large-hearted and patient with our fellowmen?

For one, I am very happy that in his description of what God is like Jesus included this parable about the unmerciful servant who failed in God's test of the sincerity of his plea for forgiveness. So this is a call for forgiveness. "So whatever you wish that men would do to you, do so to them (Matt. 7:12)." A forgiving God requires those who receive that forgiveness to be forgiving in turn.

PART III
OUR GIVING GOD

CHAPTER 9
HIMSELF

It is the thesis of this section that if one is to understand even in part the kind of a One that God is, one has to understand him in terms of his gifts to men. And he was and is and ever shall be giving gifts to his children. If you want one text for this whole section, though each chapter shall have a specific text, that allover text would be from Romans 8:32: "He who did not spare his own Son but gave him up for us all, will he not also give us all things with him?" We do have a "giving God," and just as we parents give good gifts and supply needs to our children because of our love for them, so he gives good gifts to us because we are precious to him. Here we must never forget or become confused—he loves us not because we merit it, or because we earn it, or because we love and serve him. It is the other way around. "We love because he first loved us." "In this is love, not that we loved God but that he loved us and sent his Son to be the expiation for our sins."

The giving God. The Statement of Faith of the United Church of Christ really is built around this idea. The statement refers to his gifts as the deeds of God. "We believe in God the eternal spirit, Father of our Lord Jesus Christ and our Father and to his deeds we testify." Well, those deeds are because of his love, are an expression of his love, are the proof of his love. In this section that love is explicated by some of the gifts that God presents because of that love. He gives us himself. Unless he did this, all the rest he gives would be as dust and ashes. If he gave us the most valuable gifts but withheld himself, so that we could not know him and he did not know us, so we could not have fellowship with him and so he did not (to use the phrase which is used about Moses), "speak . . . face to face, as a man speaks to his friend (Exod. 33:11)"—all his other gifts would be as nothing. God's greatest gift to us is himself, so that he no longer is the great mystery, the great enigma, but our friend. Now, of course, God is greater than our understanding, even as a mother or a father is greater than the understanding of a little child; but the child does know the parent, even if only partially. So God reveals himself to us, so that though he is greater than our minds, yet we do know him at least in part.

He reveals himself to us through the Word. It could be said that he reveals himself to us through the Bible and that would be true too, but that would imply that every word in the Bible, every sentence, every paragraph was as accurate and adequate a picture of God as every other one. That, when you study the Book, actually is not true. A lot of the customs, the mores, the folkways, the ignorance of the people and their times made their way into the Bible; and if you are going to rightly interpret the Word, you have to take that into account.

The following is one good illustration out of the language of the Book. You know that the New Testament was written in Greek. Paul, who was a university-trained man and knew good Greek, wrote his letters in excellent Greek. The writer of the Gospel of John, on the other hand, had not had the opportunity for such excellent training. So he wrote in the Greek he knew, which is filled with Hebraisms—that is, the taking of a Hebrew or Aramaic word and putting a Greek ending on it, to make it seem like a Greek word. The fact that these men were writing for what later became a part of the scriptural canon does not mean that they wrote in a language they had not mastered. So it is with other facets of their learning and understanding. (Their understanding of evil spirits is a good example.)

But all this does not make the record any less valuable. It only underscores the fact that it is necessary to read the scriptures from the point of view and the background of the day in which they were written and the experiences of those who wrote them. Or, to put it a bit differently, the Bible—all of it, from cover to cover, including the covers—is not the Word of God, it contains the word of God. It contains the message that God was trying to get through to men, but that word was sometimes constricted and hampered by the understanding, the language, the beliefs of the men through whom the Word was revealed. Take a few of the psalms for instance, where the writers were calling down the wrath of God upon their enemies. Certainly that is a bit different from the spirit of the New Testament, the teachings of our Lord. But you have to understand that that was the kind of vengeful faith these writers had, and they could not keep it out of their writing. In short, all the Bible writers composed out of the spirit and understanding of their day. The Bible is not all the Word of God. The Bible contains the Word, and therefore you do not have to defend to the death every jot and tittle of it. The wonder is that it is as accurate and as applicable to this different age as it is. The wonder of it is that God got his message through to men as plainly and as precisely as he did. But enough of this.

The real question is how well acquainted are we with the way God has revealed himself to us in the word? That revelation has no worth at all, unless it is transmitted to our hearts and minds. Actually, it might as well not be in the Book unless it finally gets into us. And this is where my chief concern rests these days. There seems so little effort on our part to study the word, and sometimes so little concern on the part of the church to transmit the word. And yet it is through the word that God reveals himself to us. For too many of us God is some hypothetical, nebulous spirit off in some "wild blue yonder" about whom we know precious little. And all the time we have the word—the Book, which reveals God's dealing with his people, his people's understanding of him. And yet for too many of us it is a Book we never crack. To be sure, it is not an easy Book to read and understand. But that does not stop us in any other field. I know enough about science texts to know they are not easy to understand. A history is not child's play to read. Engineering texts read not easily. Law books are as dry as dust. Yet that does not stop us from pursuing such knowledge. But if we cannot understand the scripture on the first reading we lay it aside and give up the struggle. Yet in the Book is the basic knowledge about the God who created the heavens and the earth. In the Book God reveals himself in what he has done, is doing, and yet shall do. Yet far too many of us are actually unacquainted with what is written there. It is my honest belief that never will we have a strong faith or a strong church until as a church and as individual Christians we pay more attention to spiritual nurture; and that begins with a knowledge of the word. In church, God makes himself known to us in the word.

In the second place, he makes himself known to us in Jesus Christ. Do you remember the Master's words: "He who has seen me has seen the Father (John 14:9)"? This is one of the two most important facets of the ministry of Jesus to us. The other, of course, is the atonement through which our forgiveness and salvation are provided. But in a way even prior to that in importance is the revelation of the Father by the Son. Up to the coming of Jesus, men had never really been able to be sure what God was like. They had tried to push back the curtain, they had tried to imagine—but certainty was not for them. Then came Jesus, walking and talking, teaching and healing, loving and serving; and men began to say to themselves, God ought to be like that—and then God is like that. Oh yes, of course, God is more than we can see in Jesus. But that is not only because when the Word became flesh there were certain limits which the humanity of Jesus imposed upon the deity of the Master, but also because he was too much for our small minds to comprehend or our small eyes to see.

Let's go at it another way. If you were given the power to make a God the way you wanted him (if that does not seem too irreverent), how different would you make him in spirit, in goals, and in techniques from what you find in Jesus Christ? Oh yes, because he would be living today, in a different environment, the stories he would tell to illustrate the truth he was teaching would be different, have different settings; he would dress differently, live differently, travel in a different manner—but essentially the highest and best that we know is exemplified, is revealed, in the life of Jesus Christ. God is like Jesus.

Think what a milestone in human history, in man's search for God, is marked by the event which is described in the Gospel according to John: "And the Word became flesh and dwelt among us, full of grace and truth; we have beheld his glory, glory as of the only Son from the Father." He who had been hid and distorted by man's understanding or misunderstanding, so that sometimes he was unrecognizable, now became plain because his spirit, his justice, his love, his forgiveness, his patience dwelled in a man. All of God that one can possibly cram into a man, dwelled in Jesus Christ. No longer did men have to wonder, now they knew—for they saw God in his Son. They saw him telling men how they should live, how they should devote themselves to meeting the needs of their fellows; they learned what sacrifice was like and what it did; they learned what love was and is and ever shall be —they saw God. God made himself known to men in Jesus Christ.

But perhaps best of all, God makes himself known to us as we walk with him, as we do his will, as we accomplish his purpose, and as we try to meet the needs of our neighbors. How do we know what God is like, what he will do for us, how he stands ready to help us? How do we know? Well, in the final analysis we become certain, as we try out the Christian way, as we allow him to live within us and as we live within him. This is the pragmatic test: does it work? Is there power in God that is available to men? Is there any difference between the men who follow in the way and those who do not? What does history claim and to what does it attest? You can begin almost anywhere you want to begin.

Let's begin with the apostles. What kind of men were they? The only adequate description of them is that they were very simple men, uneducated, unlearned, economically poor, without status and position. And what happened to them? They were with Jesus for three years, and then they went out to change the world, and that is exactly what they did! Frank Mead, years ago, wrote *They Marched Across the World*. And they did. Surely no one would have been willing to wager anything on the fact that they would leave an impact upon the world; but they really exploded across the miles, until the whole world was different because of them. They were opposed by the Roman government, and "Rome ruled the world." Yet nothing could stay them. Paul said, after he had a chance to try this out, "I can do all things in him who strengthens me (Phil. 4:13)"—and his life proved it. This matter of being doubted on every hand and yet successful reminds me of one part of the *Ballad for Americans*. Talking about the American dream of freedom, the song goes:

Nobody who was anybody believed it,
Everybody who was anybody, they doubted it,

And they are doubting still
And I guess they always will.*

Yet in spite of everything going against it, the dream succeeded. And you can come right down through the years.

In less than 250 years that little band of Christians had made such an impact upon Rome that the cross was emblazoned upon the banners of the Eternal City. It was true that the blood of those martyrs had become the seed of the church. There was Polycarp, who when he was given one last chance to recant before being burned at the stake, said, "Eighty and six years have I served my Lord. How can I deny him now?" There were Francis of Assisi, and Luther, Zwingli, Calvin, Knox, Beza, and Farrell. There were Brewster and John Robinson, there were Hooker, Bushnell, the Wesleys, Coke and Asbury, Otterbein and Jonathan Edwards—there was Washington at Valley Forge, and Lincoln during the desperate days of the War Between the States. Not too many of these were really great men in their own right. But all of them became great as they served their Lord, as he lived within them.

But the real test is what happens to you and to me as we try to walk the ways of earth with him. Is he only a mirage, are the phrases only high-sounding words; or do they speak forth the reality of the universe? "I will not leave you desolate; I will come to you (John 14:18)." "Go therefore and make disciples of all nations, baptizing them in the name of the Father and of the Son and of the Holy Spirit, teaching them to observe all that I have commanded you; and lo, I am with you always, to the close of

---

* John Latouche, *Ballad for Americans.* Copyright © 1940, Renewed 1967 Robbins Music Corporation. Used by permission. (*Ballad for Americans* is not merely a song of doubt, however. The text states at great length that the majority of the people who make up the body politic "believed it.")

the age (Matt. 28:19-20)." The real testimony is that which is given today by people like us, who know full well their shortcomings and their weaknesses, their lack of power and strength—people like us who become great in the service of God because we let him reveal himself to us, but more, because his power and strength flow into our living.

Most of you know this, because it has happened to you, it has happened within you. This is the real way a man comes to know for a certainty that God is real and that his power is available. That it is not merely like a suit to be put on and worn, but like a new heart within the depth of his soul. Do not think all the really great things happened in the dim, distant past. There are plenty of miracles that take place today, only we seldom hear about them; about the miracle that comes to pass when a one-talented person gives himself wholly to God and does great things in the world—deeds he never would have dreamed he could do! Deeds that make a difference in the way people can live and enjoy the great world in which we dwell, that provide healing for those diseased, food for those who starve, hope for those who are full of despair. And it is all because of the revelation of God to men—not even in a Book, though it is there; not even in Christ, though, of course, it is there in all its fullness; but in you and me. Nobody can doubt that. It is the convincing proof of what God is like.

I suppose every one of us would choose a different attribute of God to emphasize. Actually we ourselves at different times would choose different attributes. On one day we are impressed with this gift and on another day with that one. In this section we are putting the emphasis upon the great gifts of God to men. If he is anything at all, he is a giving God. And first among the things which he gives to men is himself. He might have remained aloof, having no truck with us, letting us imagine what he is like—and all imagining something different. But he did not. He revealed himself to us, so that we would know, could be sure, so that he would be no stranger, so that we might meet him and know him and be sustained by this faith and knowledge in the rough-and-tumble life. He calls us by his name, because we are his; because he is our Father and we are his children. And the children know the father in a way that no one else does.

We have a giving God. He gives us himself.

CHAPTER 10
HIS
WORLD

We are proceeding on the assumption that if one is to know God then one has to know him in the expression of his love to and for men. You know that love best when you look at his great gifts. This chapter will discuss that love as it is revealed in the gift of his world.

We do live in a wonderful world, more wonderful than we sometimes understand. The world is filled these days with so much disorder, selfishness, bloodshed, trouble, and suffering that it often blinds us to the glory of our universe. The text for this chapter is from Genesis 1:31: "And God saw everything that he had made, and behold, it was very good. And there was evening and there was morning, a sixth day." We must never forget that if we are to judge correctly about the wonderfulness of his world we have to remember how he created it, in contrast to the way we have despoiled it. We do have a giving God—and he has given us an amazingly wonderful world. He saw everything that he had made and behold, it was very good.

First of all, it is a world of beauty and bounty. One need not emphasize this if we open our eyes to see what is before us; if we go out into the country and see the way the world looks when we have not overrun it and ravished it with concrete, brick, and mortar. I remember being in the home of a professional photographer whose wife made a hobby of taking close-up pictures of single blossoms—the camera being usually no more than four or six inches away from the flower. That night looking at her slides I saw what I had never seen before or since: the heart of a flower. It was beauty magnified. Another time I saw, as many of you have, the Norwegian fjords with their breathtaking waterfalls—not just a single fall at a glance, but a dozen or more, falling usually about three thousand feet. Or the beauty of the Tetons as mirrored against Jenny Lake. You name it, and it is all there. A beautiful world to behold! Rivers and lakes, growing grain and grazing cattle, waterfalls and rapids, the beauty of the dawn and the majesty—frightening majesty—of a summer storm. What more need I say? A rose kissed by the dew and the flame of red poppies. A world of beauty, if only we take time to look.

The world is not only beautiful but bountiful. Before the ecologists scared us to death I often said that God always provided his gifts in abundance. There is the little boy in straitened circumstances who on his first glimpse of the sea said, "Well, I am glad to see something of which there is enough." I remember well on my first ocean crossing, I was nonplussed every day because there was always water beyond. During the Second World War I had read many times how the Japanese and the American fleets, in the midst of a battle, would lose each other. I just could not understand that until I saw the ocean, many times shrouded in fog, and all that water. Enough air to breathe if only we do not pollute it completely, enough food to eat if we could learn how to distribute it properly. I am not quite as pessimistic as some people. While it is true that today the population is increasing geometrically and the food supply in arithmetical ratio, I think this problem can be solved. Enough. In bountiful proportions. Like the two fishes and five loaves—enough and to spare.

And what wonders there are for us to learn still! In the time when some of us have lived we have seen the great revolutions in the electrical world, the communication world (I made my first radio the summer after I graduated from high school, and it was not a crystal set either)—television with the use of the satellites, so there is instant transmission around the world—and the medical world: pneumonia shackled, polio all but wiped out, diphtheria and scarlet fever almost forgotten. And the end is not yet. In fact, we have only made a beginning. And do not forget all this was possible "when the morning stars sang together," if we had only learned the secrets stored up in this beautiful and wonderful and bountiful world. Surely, God has given us as his love gift this great world in which we live. And never let the disorder and trouble of our age blind you to the wonder of nature. Oh yes, nature can be cruel as well as friendly, but look at all the ways to control the cruel side of nature we have already learned—and we shall learn more, of this I am confident.

All of which leads me to my next point. This is a world of precision. We were returning from Florida in March 1970 when an eclipse of the sun occurred. I am not sure how long before the event the time of the eclipse had been predicted to the second, but a long time. At least they told us another would not occur for almost one hundred years. The shadow of the moon on the sun began at exactly the time it had been predicted; and all this was possible because this is the precise world—no caprice about it. Well, the point is that the advances which we have witnessed have been made because the universe is not changeable but always reacts in the same way. What if once out of one hundred times water ran uphill instead of downhill, or every second Tuesday two bodies would not attract each other in direct proportion to their size and in inverse proportion to the distance between them? Don't you see that no so-called laws of nature—which is only a statement of the way nature acts invariably—could be formulated in a capricious world? You throw a ball into the air and it comes down every time unless some intervening force is exerted. The same is true of the first of the month and February 29 in leap years. The very fact we have leap years is because the travel of the earth around the sun can be charted a century or two in advance.

Now, this is not all to the good. There are some disadvantages to it, but they are a million times over-balanced by the advantages. I lose my footing on a ladder and fall to the ground every time, whether I have been in church last Sunday or not, whether I beat my wife or we live happily together. One of the tasks that every minister has to face is trying to explain to a family why an accident happened—and that such an accident had nothing at all to do with the character of the man or the woman who was the victim. The son of one of our friends was walking down the streets of Washington—the nation's capital— and out of nowhere came a bullet, and he was in the path of that bullet. The fact that he was a good boy did not affect the course of that death-dealing instrument. But would you want to live in a universe where bullets went off their course to kill the bad and spare the good? Don't you see—of course you do—that all the good things we have are because, to use Christ's words, "for he makes his sun rise on the evil and on the good, and sends rain on the just and on the unjust (Matt. 5:45) "? This is a precise world, and all of science, all of technology, all of our inventions are posited upon that truth. You can't have your cake and eat it too. We like to ride in airplanes; this is possible because the laws of aerodynamics are fixed and engineers can build upon them. If they make a mistake and a strut collapses, we read about it in the paper, even if the plane is filled with saints. This is a precise world, where phenomena occur as cause and effect. We cut the timber, denuding the hills and valleys, and we have dust storms and floods—no matter who cuts the timber, saints or sinners. One leaves as devastating a trail behind as the other. Precision is the basis of all our science and all our technological advances. God has given us such a universe.

He has given us a world in which men are free, free even to disobey him and his moral law. The greatest dignity a man possesses is the freedom of choice that God vouchsafes to him. God even will not violate the freedom of his people in order to save them, to bring them back again to his house and home. There is much which could be said about forgiveness. Suffice it to say that in the parable of the prodigal son, the boy had to come to himself first before the father could help. In the parable the father is God and the boy is we. What if everything you did was determined for you, by your friend, by your enemy, by the government, even by God? There would be no credit for the good you do, no blame for the evil. You could not help yourself. When you come right down to it, this is God's greatest gift to us—that he made us free; that he gave us the right to chart our own course; that we can say yes or no to everyone.

Now, such a gift carries along with it great responsibility. There have been many times when personally I would have been glad to be able to blame some wrong decision of mine on somebody else—but sitting where I sat I could not do that. To use Harry Truman's phrase (which he is supposed to have had on his desk in the White House), "Here is where the buck stops." Well, I had eight years of that, and it was not always pleasant. But I submit to you that it was more pleasant than being a puppet with someone else pulling the strings.

Freedom carries responsibilities. Do you remember some of the first times when you entrusted some hard decisions to your children? That meant that they could decide either rightly or wrongly—and there really was nothing you could do to get them out of the consequences of their decision. The Herbsters have two daughters. When they were much younger than they now are— (the older one was perhaps a senior in high school), the older one particularly was doing very well in sewing. And there was nothing she liked to do more than to visit the yard goods department in a store and look at and sometimes buy material for a dress. On this particular occasion the two girls had been given their mother's credit card for a purchase —and after they had made this purchase they ended up as usual in the yard goods department. There the older girl saw some of the most beautiful material she ever had seen. So she went to the pattern department, selected a way to make a dress, found out how much material was required, and then went back and made the purchase, never asking the price of the material. When the clerk gave her the bill she was astounded and frightened. I am not sure what she thought I would do to her. At least she came home and confessed and was contrite. After we had talked it over I said to her, "I guess it was very good that you had this experience and learned this lesson while your father was still paying your bills and not your husband." I tell you this homely illustration because decision does carry with it great responsibility. But who of us would want to escape the responsibility by giving up our freedom?

There is another side to all this. If God made us all free, who are we to impinge upon the freedom of other people? What we treasure so much we ought to allow others to enjoy also. This has something very definite to say to us these days about equality, about civil, economic, and social righteousness, about the Third World that is so disinherited. I certainly do not have to draw that picture for you. Eugene Debs said it a long time ago: "While there is a lower class I am in it, while there is a criminal element I am of it; while there is a soul in prison, I am not free." We are all in this thing together, and if freedom is threatened anywhere, it is threatened and undermined everywhere. We cannot keep our freedom unless and until everyone is free. What we want to enjoy we must vouchsafe to every man, woman, and child. There is no other way. If God made this world and his children to be free, we must not—in the long run, we cannot—alter that course. We dare not take his gift from any of his children. That is the reason why the issues of the day are so important, and why we as followers of the Lord cannot be uncommitted in these days. This is why we must take a stand. We have no more right to destroy the freedom that God has provided for all men than we have to pollute and despoil his universe. In Galatians, Paul writes, "For freedom Christ has set us free; stand fast therefore, and do not submit again to a yoke of slavery (5:1)." And he could as well have added, Do not submit to a yoke of slavery for yourself or for any other man. We were created to be free, and free men will be, whether we approve or not. Freedom is in our genes; we imbibe it with our mother's milk and with the air we breathe. This is a wonderful world, and one of its finest attributes is the freedom that was meant for all men and women and children, regardless of race, color, culture, language, or past conditions of servitude. We were meant to be free.

And finally, God created this old world with a moral order at its heart that is as unchangeable and immutable as the physical order of the universe. This world was built with righteousness, justice, love at its heart, and one violates them with the same tragic results as when one violates the law of gravity or of electrical energy. In fact, one does not violate the law of gravity, one only illustrates it. So it is with the moral order of the world. One does not violate it except one reaps the result of such violation. Paul has a lot to say about this: "For he who sows to his own flesh will from the flesh reap corruption; but he who sows to the Spirit will from the Spirit reap eternal life. And let us not grow weary in well-doing, for in due season we shall reap, if we do not lose heart (Gal. 6:8-9)." That verse reminds me of a quip which I read many years ago and which I have repeated up and down the church, so that I realize many of you have heard it; but it is so appropriate that I must repeat it now. "The reason why the kingdom tarries so long is because the good people get tired of being good faster than the bad people get tired of being bad."

This is a morally precise world—as morally precise as it is physically precise. But so many of us are so slow to understand that. We think we can do evil or think evil and that it has no effect upon our living, upon our character. How far from the truth that is. The evil that we let loose in the world inevitably comes back to us. It may take a few days or a few months or a few years, but it does come back. Be sure of that. There is no need to argue the point or illustrate it. I simply lay it out to you. You cannot steal, you cannot lie, you cannot kill and not have to reap the results. Nor can you hate or be full of lust or be full of selfishness or self-centeredness or greed or impatience without its taking a toll of your living. On the other hand, you cannot build into your life large-heartedness, love, compassion, and patience without these virtues making a difference in you and in your living. The one is as true as the other, and both as true as the law of gravity. We were meant for love, not for hatred, for goodwill not ill will; and one practices the latter at one's peril. Do you remember the story of "The Great Stone Face"? Ernest was born and reared within the shadow of the "face," and from his earliest days had learned of the legend that someday one who looked like the profile would come back into the valley. Every day Ernest thought about this, every day the lines of that face became more familiar to Ernest, until one day the valley was surprised (yet it ought to have been no surprise at all) to see that Ernest himself resembled the "face." It was inevitable that so it would be. "Whatever a man sows, that he will also reap (Gal. 6:7)."

Really, this is a great world we live in, much greater than our fathers ever knew, and by that same token much greater than we know! And it is surely one of God's most precious gifts to us. We have a giving God—he gives us his world, a world of wonder and precision.

CHAPTER 11
FORGIVENESS

What if a man never had a chance to start a new day, a new chapter of his life, to make a new beginning? What if —after acting like a selfish, self-centered person against those who love us most—we could not sidle up to them and say, "I'm sorry, please forgive me," and know that even before we said the words, forgiveness was extended to us. Furthermore, in the light of what we learned from that and out of the magnanimity of our friends, we have been able to start out anew. Life certainly would be a bitter experience without these new beginnings. If these be our experiences in our relationship with our fellows, how much more must they be necessary in our relationship with the eternal God and Father of us all. It is from such chapters of tragedy and joy that we begin to study together.

The text is from Romans 5:20, where the apostle Paul is talking about sin and grace. And right here I had better stop to define the word grace. It has so many meanings that we are often a bit confused—particularly when one of the meanings, the particular one used in the context we are discussing, is a bit obsolete. In other words, we really do not use the word grace much anymore. When we do use it, we mean attractiveness, charm, beauty, suppleness. While that is a very worthwhile description of grace, it is hardly what Paul is talking about. Grace, in the sense in which he uses the word, is the unmerited favor of God. It means mercy, forgiveness, compassion. It means that God gives to us, not because we earn it or deserve it, but because of his love. It is like our relations with our children. Sometimes we say, "You are forgiven before you ask." And true that is. We love our children so much that we want to bridge the chasm which their disobedience causes; because of our love for them, we forgive them quickly and fully.

Now back to the text. The King James Version reads: "But where sin abounded, grace did much more abound." The Revised Standard Version reads: "But where sin increased, grace abounded all the more." J. B. Phillips translates the Greek in a way that it seems to have a little clearer implication. "Yet, though sin is shown to be wide and deep, thank God his grace is wider and deeper still!" The giving God. His grace, his forgiveness. To repeat, what if one could not be sure of the forgiveness of God? What if one had to live out his whole life under the weight of sin? What if one did not have the assurance that though "sin is shown to be wide and deep, thank God his grace is wider and deeper still"?

Or let us put it into an altogether different context. What if you never heard the words "For God so loved the world that he gave his only Son, that whoever believes in him should not perish but have eternal life." You know, there is such a thing as becoming too accustomed to some of the great gifts which we have. We tend to begin to take them for granted. In these latter days ecologists are beginning to scream that unless we take care we shall not always have enough pure air to breathe, enough pure water to drink, and enough blue sky through which the sun can shine. Most of us never gave the worth of these gifts much thought. We simply took them as a matter of course. We did not think of them as the gift of God, as a trust to care for responsibly. In the same way, we have heard these great words so often that they no longer make a great impact upon our minds and hearts. I sat the other day for a while, trying to imagine how I would feel if I had never heard them. Paul talks about this in one of his other letters, about men "without God and without hope in this world." You really cannot imagine what life would be like without the promise which John 3:16 contains. But at least I tried, and life looked very dark. And then I tried to imagine the change that would come about if for the first time, the very first time, I heard the words "For God so loved the world that he gave his only Son, that whoever believes in him should not perish but have eternal life." The best clue to what this would mean was how bright the electric lights looked when they came on again the night of the great blackout in the northeast. You never appreciate what light really is and does and makes possible until you are without it. The giving God—I daresay among his greatest gifts is his forgiveness. "Though sin is shown to be wide and deep, thank God his grace is wider and deeper still."

It ought not be necessary to labor the point that sin is wide and deep—and everywhere, even within us. I graduated from seminary in the spring of 1929. We were pretty sure then that the millennium, the kingdom, utopia, was just around the corner. We were on an escalator of progress—give us just a few more years and we would be there. War, disease, hunger, ignorance, man's cussedness would be obliterated forever. Well, even then we were on the verge of the Great Depression, and over the hill beyond was the Second World War, then the nuclear age (which has so much in it for good and for ill), and now whatever you would call these days of crime, violence, war, starvation, selfishness. No one believes sincerely today that progress is automatic or that we are approaching utopia. We are too well acquainted with the disastrous consequences of sin in all of human life to at all minimize what our fathers so aptly and truthfully set forth. We know something about sin—sin against God and sin against our fellows.

But there is one aspect of this that may not be so clear, and that is that the sin in the world so easily and so quickly gets into us. Someone wrote once that the best defense against sin is always to be shocked by it. He had hold of a truth. Part of our trouble today is that we have lived so close to the sin that is in the world, that we are no longer shocked by it. We have come to the place where some of us could be said to have made peace with the sin of the world. The old singer of the Hebrews saw the danger in this when he wrote, "Ye that love the Lord, hate evil (Ps. 97:10, KJV)."

Beyond this, we sometimes fail to see that the essence of sin is the attitude we have, and not necessarily the deeds we do—an evil mind and an evil heart will eventually lead one into an evil course of action. Jesus put his finger on this when he spoke concerning the dietary practice of his brethren of the Hebrew faith. The scribes and Pharisees had come to Jesus to criticize his disciples because they did not keep every jot and tittle of the dietary laws. After he had answered them adequately, he called his disciples to him and said:

Hear and understand: not what goes into the mouth defiles a man, but what comes out of the mouth, this defiles a man. . . . Do you not see that whatever goes into the mouth passes into the stomach, and so passes on? But what comes out of the mouth proceeds from the heart, and this defiles a man. For out of the heart come evil thoughts, murder, adultery, fornication, theft, false witness, slander. These are what defile a man; but to eat with unwashed hands does not defile a man.
—Matthew 15:10-11, 17-20

99

Or there is the plain teaching of the Sermon on the Mount:

> You have heard that it was said, "An eye for an eye and a tooth for a tooth." But I say to you, Do not resist one who is evil. . . . You have heard that it was said to the men of old, "You shall not kill; and whoever kills shall be liable to judgment." But I say to you that every one who is angry with his brother shall be liable to judgment. . . . You have heard that it was said, "You shall not commit adultery." But I say to you that every one who looks at a woman lustfully has already committed adultery with her in his heart.
>
> —Matthew 5:38-39, 21, 27-28

It was out of this background that a beloved professor used to say, "If you are going to fight against sin, you have to do it in the imagination stage." Is that not very accurate?

We do not have much trouble with what could be termed the grosser sins. We do not steal, we do not get drunk, we never killed anyone. We do not run around with somebody else's wife. But if the essence of sin is not only these but the sin which one even tries to hide from oneself, if getting angry is murder (to oneself and to one's brother), if lustful thoughts are the seed of immorality, if covetousness, greed, jealousy, and gossip are also sin— then we stand not pure but convicted. No wonder the publican prayed, "God, be merciful to me a sinner (Luke 18:13)!" and Paul wrote, "Christ Jesus came into the world to save sinners. And I am the foremost of sinners (1 Tim. 1:15)." Let us not fool ourselves—the sin that is in the world is in us too.

If that were all there is to say, then perhaps one ought to seal one's lips. But that is not the whole story; in fact, it is only the beginning of the story—a sorry beginning to be sure, but only the beginning. "Though sin is shown to be wide and deep, thank God his grace is wider and deeper still." The giving God, forgiveness.

The truth is that the gospel is not about sin, though of course if there were no sin, there would be no need of forgiveness; it is the story of the fullness of forgiveness that makes the news "good news." It is forgiveness that is the burden of the gospel, or should we say the joy of the gospel. Listen to some of these sentences that always seem so surprising and so amazing to the people who read them. Romans 1:15-16: "So I am eager to preach the gospel to you also who are in Rome. For I am not ashamed of the gospel: it is the power of God for salvation to every one who has faith, to the Jew first and also the Greek." Acts 10:42-43: "And he commanded us to preach to the people, and to testify that he is the one ordained by God to be judge of the living and the dead. To him all the prophets bear witness that every one who believes in him receives forgiveness of sins through his name." Acts 13:38-39: "Let it be known to you therefore, brethren, that through this man forgiveness of sins is proclaimed to you, and by him every one that believes is freed from everything from which you could not be freed by the law of Moses." Luke 23:34: "And Jesus said, 'Father, forgive them; for they know not what they do.'" Luke 19:10: "For the Son of man came to seek and to save the lost." The Old Testament records: "For I have no pleasure in the death of any one, says the Lord God; so turn, and live (Ezek. 18:32)."

The story of the coming of Jesus is the working out of that desire and purpose of God. That is the reason it is called the gospel. Of course, the two best stories which Jesus told illustrating this great gift of God are the lost sheep and the lost son. Since these have been treated in another context, they will not be repeated here. But what is said here is that "the name of the game" is forgiveness, the return of the wayward to the Father's heart and home. When we turn to him he forgives, and he says, "Boy, you're home; thank God, you are home!"

What a heavenly Father we have. One who does not allow our sin—and sin is a despicable thing—our sin to separate us from him, but one who forgives fully, freely, and abundantly. Why then do we shut ourselves out from his great forgiveness? Why then do some of us live as if forgiveness, God's forgiveness, were not available, possible, as if he were not eager to forgive us? It is hard to understand that, is it not—except for our stubbornness and our stupid independence? Sometimes it seems that if there were something we could do, like lying on a bed of spikes or measuring a mile by prostrating our body consecutively on the ground, some people would be more willing to accept forgiveness. But to be so humbled as to have to admit that there is nothing that we can do to earn mercy and pardon, that we simply have to accept it as a child accepts gifts from his parents, is a bitter pill to swallow. We want to keep on thinking and saying that we are self-made men—beholden to no one. And all the time we have a God who loves us so much that he allows nothing on his part to keep us from him.

The thing that is of great concern is that we should come to have a new and a greater appreciation for the kind of a God in whom we believe. He is not some vindictive, vengeful, ruthless, punitive, stonyhearted one, who delights in the sufferings of his people. He is not like Jonah of old, who wanted to see God burn up the city of Nineveh and all the people in it. God, our God, is a God of mercy and love, tenderhearted, forgiving us again and again and again. That, of course, does not mean that we should presume upon that forgiveness. That mistake has been made many times in the long history of our faith. But it does mean that whenever we turn to him he will receive us with welcome and joy; or better still, he will be out on the trails of life trying to call us back unto him.

Dr. Paul Scherer writes in one of his older books about the fact that one does not have to look God up once a week as if he were hard to find. He says that God steps out from around every corner to confront us with his love and his compassion. He is in a hurry to forgive his people.

Our giving God. Forgiveness. "Though sin be wide and deep, thank God His grace is wider and deeper still."

CHAPTER 12
HE
GIVES US
THE GOOD LIFE

In a sense we are now approaching the most misunderstood and the most unkept of all the relationships of the Christian life. We have been speaking of knowing God, understanding him and the truth for which he stands, by attending to his gifts to men. We talked about the gifts of himself and of his world and of his forgiveness; and we have tried to make it plain that each of these, and all of them together, have come to us, not because we earn them or merit them or actually deserve them, but rather because of his love for us. "For by grace you have been saved through faith; and this is not your own doing, it is the gift of God—not because of works, lest any man should boast (Eph. 2:8-9)." We come to the Christian way; how and why we ought to live that Christian way. We ought to live it, not to get the favor of God—that we already have—but to show forth our gratitude to him for his love and his forgiveness to us. The catechism in which we were reared makes it so plain:

That I belong—body and soul, in life and in death —not to myself but to my faithful Savior, Jesus Christ, who at the cost of his own blood has fully paid for all my sins and has completely freed me from the dominion of the devil; that he protects me so well that without the will of my Father in heaven not a hair can fall from my head; indeed, that everything must fit his purpose for my salvation. Therefore, by his Holy Spirit, he also assures me of eternal life, and makes me wholeheartedly willing and ready from now on to live for him.*

The catechism goes on:

It is not only a certain knowledge by which I accept as true all that God has revealed to us in his Word, but also a wholehearted trust which the Holy Spirit creates in me through the gospel, that, not only to others, but to me also God has given the forgiveness of sins, everlasting righteousness and salvation, out of sheer grace solely for the sake of Christ's saving work.†

And yet so many people do not seem to lay hold of this logic. In spite of all that is in the word and all the preaching and teaching, and in spite of the simple logic of our faith, many of us still think we are going to be saved because we lead "the good life." We seem to overlook some of the straightforward truths and testimony of the "great" of every age. "None is righteous, no, not one"; "Christ Jesus came into the world to save sinners. And I am the foremost of sinners." Or the words of Booker T. Washington: "We are all sinners; at least the best of us are." Let us get it right out in the open. If forgiveness, salvation, atonement, reconciliation are dependent upon our earning them by living the good life, then we are of all men most hopeless; for though we may keep the commandments, the good life is so much more than that, that the two cannot be spoken in the same breath. If we are to

---

* *The Heidelberg Catechism* (Philadelphia: United Church Press, 1962), p. 9. Copyright 1962 United Church Press.

† Ibid., p. 27.

be saved, we are saved by the love of God as that love was expressed in Jesus Christ—his life, his death, and his resurrection.

But that does not mean we are freed from the responsibility of living the Christian life. We live up to our best, Christ's best in us, as a thank offering for all he has done for us. Or to put it in another way, because of his love he gives us not only forgiveness and the assurance of eternal life, he also gives us the good life here and now; and he makes plain before us what the earmarks of that good life are.

1. He makes it plain to us that the good life is not primarily outward deeds but inward motives that eventuate in good deeds. This was so plain in the teaching of our Lord, and particularly in the Sermon on the Mount. Without at all belittling the Hebrew faith (for we must never forget that as Christians we stem from that faith), it is simply fact that the Hebrew faith stressed men's outward deeds without putting adequate emphasis upon the motives underneath the deeds. And so with some Hebrews it became almost a game to see how much one could keep the outward letter of the law, and yet at the same time violate the spirit of the law. It was all this that constantly kept Jesus in conflict with the scribes and Pharisees. Illustrations can be multiplied. Escaping the tithe by saying that income or property is devoted to the care of our parents. Resisting the desire to kill but harboring hatred and anger deep within the heart. Being outwardly true to a wife but having a roving and lustful eye. Keeping all the ceremonial laws of the Hebrew faith, but having a heart filled with unrighteousness and injustice. Whole volumes of interpretations were written by Hebrew scholars to make it plain what the faith taught a man could and could not do, but these volumes were of no worth when men really were not sincere. Sincerity is the important thing—not how little but how much. De-

sire to keep the law, not finding ways to escape it, was the essence. For the kingdom is not eating or drinking, or keeping the laws regarding eating or drinking, but righteousness and peace in the Holy Spirit.

But this effort to make law the essential thing did not end with that generation. Think for a moment of all the subterfuges which we use to counter this plain teaching of our Lord. "No one will ever find out!" "I am as good as my neighbor." "I keep all the commandments." "No one ever expects me to be perfect." "I go to church every Sunday and I give generously of my income." And all the time our life is filled with greed, with hatred, with prejudice, with lust, with jealousy, with unfair criticism. These are the important things, so says Christ, and not our outward acts. Oh yes, outward acts are important too, but they stem from attitudes of heart and mind. The logic is plain: if one harbors evil thoughts and attitudes in one's heart, it will not be long until they result in evil deeds. Jesus says, "For out of the heart come evil thoughts, murder, adultery, fornication, theft, false witness, slander (Matt. 15:19)." The important thing is the spirit by which we live, the motives which drive us on, that sometimes consume our whole being. If our motives are right, the deeds take care of themselves.

2. The second principle which our Lord lays down is that love of God and love of neighbor must be the basis for the good life—nothing short of these. Do you remember the circumstances surrounding Christ's summing up of the ten commandments in two? The Pharisees, those leaders of the church who put great stress upon appearances, on outward law-keeping, upon how they appeared in the eyes of their fellows, plotted to see what Jesus would say to their question concerning which was the greatest and most important law. He immediately summed it all in the easy-to-repeat, but hard-to-live formula: "You shall love the Lord your God with all your

heart, and with all your soul, and with all your mind. This is the great and first commandment. And a second is like it, You shall love your neighbor as yourself. On these two commandments depend all the law and the prophets (Matt. 22:37-40)." The epistles—and particularly the first epistle of John—then goes on to make plain the motivation of our love for God and for our fellowmen:

> In this is love, not that we loved God but that he loved us and sent his Son to be the expiation for our sins. . . . We love, because he first loved us. If any one says, "I love God," and hates his brother, he is a liar; for he who does not love his brother whom he has seen, cannot love God whom he has not seen. And this commandment we have from him, that he who loves God should love his brother also.
>
> —1 John 4:10, 19-21

In short, our love for God and for our neighbor stems from and is a response to God's love for us.

Let me put it just as bluntly and plainly as it can be expressed. If a man were to walk down Main Street of any city, town, or village and ask each person whom he meets if he loves God, there would be few who would say no. But if we then tested out the profession of that love with a review of the evidence of whether he loves his neighbor, whether he treats all men as brothers, I fear we would in many cases get an altogether different answer. Dare we, right now, put those very two questions to ourselves? Do we love God? And what evidence is there to prove that we love God if the test is how much love we have for our fellowman?

"And who is my neighbor (Luke 10:29)?" "Everyone who has need of your help," came back the unmistakable answer. Or there was that other train of logic which Jesus gave us in the parable of the last judgment. "Come, O blessed of my Father, inherit the kingdom prepared for you from the foundation of the world; for I was hungry and you gave me food, I was thirsty and you gave me drink, I was a stranger and you welcomed me, I was naked and you clothed me, I was sick and you visited me, I was in prison and you came to me (Matt. 25:34-36)." And the answer, "Truly, I say to you, as you did it to one of the least of these my brethren, you did it to me (Matt. 25:40)." How well do we stack up against these forthright and penetrating tests? Love is the pattern of the good life which God has given to us.

3. The love with which God loves us and therefore the love with which we must love our fellows is a love that holds back nothing—not even the best. In the first chapter in this section, I said that the general text for all of them would be from Romans 8:32: "He who did not spare his own Son but gave him up for us all, will he not also give us all things with him?" Dr. Paul Scherer, in one of his more recent books, catches all this up in the title of the book, which, at least for me, is unforgettable. *"Love Is a Spendthrift."* This is really what Paul talks about in 1 Corinthians 13, when he writes: "If I give away all I have, and if I deliver my body to be burned, but have not love, I gain nothing." Love holds nothing back. How many times do we only give out of our surplus? How many times do we serve only if we have nothing better or more interesting to do? How many times do we hold back the best for ourselves? Well, such is not the way to practice love according to our Lord. "He who did not spare his own Son but gave him up for us all. . . ." The father in the parable of the prodigal son did not wait for the boy to confess or ask for pardon or be rehabilitated; he ran out and received him again into his heart and his home. The shepherd in the parable of the lost sheep did not wait for the sheep to find the sheepfold; he went out,

he took risks, he expended himself "until he found it." "Having loved his own who were in the world, he loved them to the end (John 13:1)." It is the essence of love to give without measure, holding back nothing. This is the kind of love that God makes plain is the essence of the good life. This kind of love he requires of us, but he also went before us as an example.

But one thing more—and perhaps this is the most important thing of all that I shall try to say. How are we to know exactly how and when and in what way we can pour out our love upon our neighbor? The scripture makes this plain too. We call it the Golden Rule; but no matter what we call it, it is the secret of living the good life. We have to try to imagine ourselves in the situation of our fellow and then do for him what, if we were he, we would want him to do for us. *Imagine* is the key word. Sometimes to make the point really clear I call it holy imagination. And if I dare to add, I would like to say there is far too little of this in our day. I suppose that is understandable. Our own wants, our own needs, our own disappointments, our own pains are so much closer to us than the wants, needs, disappointments, and pains of the other person that we lose our perspective, and we think our own needs are so much more important. I have often put it this way: my own mosquito bites hurt me so much more than the hunger pangs, the belly retchings, of my brother, that unless I do some skillful balancing I will get the idea that my bites need more attention than his pains of starvation. Imagination, holy imagination, that is what we need. "So whatever you wish that men would do to you, do so to them (Matt. 7:12)." From a downright practical, pragmatic standpoint, our Lord never gave us more usable advice than this. How poor we would be indeed without these rules. How fortunate we are that along with the gift of himself, his world, his forgiveness, he gave us not only the principles of the good life but also a demonstration of how to achieve those principles.

Now, I have not told you anything you did not know. I do not know anything with which you are not already familiar. I have only tried to review for you some of the ways God has called us to the good life. It was also for this reason that he sent his Son. "I came that they may have life, and have it abundantly (John 10:10)." Tomorrow is a new day, or it can be for us a new day—not just another day—if and when we give ourselves, our time, our resources as a thank offering for all God has done for us. Even here he does great things for us, for he makes plain how he would have us live; and if we will, he gives us power to live that way.

CHAPTER 13
HE GIVES US
HIS MISSION
AND HIS CHURCH

We have been discussing the great gifts of God or, to express it a bit differently, our giving God, and we have spoken of the fact God gives us his world, he gives us forgiveness, the good life. Now we shall consider the fact that he gives us his mission and his church. As the Statement of Faith of the United Church of Christ expresses it: "He calls us into his church to accept the cost and joy of discipleship [notice the cost comes prior to the joy of discipleship], to be his servants in the service of men, to proclaim the gospel to all the world, and resist the powers of evil, to share in Christ's baptism and to eat at his table, to join him in his passion and victory." This is stated about as tersely and as fully as one can possibly put it. And remember this: he calls us, we do not call him.

God has a message for mankind; he has a dream to fulfill, and fulfilling that dream becomes his purpose. He wants this earth to be a decent place in which men and women and little children can live in peace and plenty. That is the way he made the earth in the beginning. Do you remember the words out of Genesis: "And God saw everything that he had made, and behold, it was very good (1:31)." But he had no sooner made it good than people began to despoil it. Look about you. Families, neighborhoods, cities, regions, countries where people could dwell together in unity—plundered and ravaged by man's inhumanity to men, by our greed, by our covetousness, by our injustice. We ravage the soil and the landscape, we pollute the water and the air; we play fast and loose with love and brotherhood. God wants that changed, and we are called to that task. He calls us, and then if we will—but never if we will not—he sends us on mission.

These days whenever I use the word mission I think I have to stop long enough to define the word, for we seem to have such distorted ideas of what mission really is and should be. The word comes from the Latin root *missio,* meaning "to send." God sends us. He wants to send us to do his will, to make his changes in the world, to proclaim the gospel and to build justice and mercy into the fabric of the way we live. He wants to send us. We have this same root meaning in our English word missive—a letter, a message which we send to another. In God's scheme of things we are to be his messengers, his couriers, his spokesmen. All of us are to be that. Certainly not just those who preach from a pulpit, but all of us who bear the name of our Lord and who have promised to walk in his ways and witness to his truth.

The truth is that we are about the most complimented people in the world. To think that God entrusts his kingdom, his dream, his purpose to us! That he calls us his partners in this great purpose! Theoretically it would be possible for God to perform a miracle and the kingdom would then come—evil would be vanquished, justice and mercy would be established. But he has not chosen that way. He decided that he would choose the slow way of asking his followers to do this for him, not intervene directly in the process. I have always been amused and intrigued by one of the stories in the Old Testament where God calls Moses to go to Egypt and say to pharaoh, "Let my people go." Do you remember the incident? Moses is keeping the flocks of his father-in-law, Jethro, and he notices a strange phenomenon, a bush seems to be burning but does not burn up. So he turns aside to see this strange happening and he hears a voice crying, "Moses, Moses!" And Moses says, "Here am I." And God continues, "I have seen the affliction of my people who are in Egypt, and have heard their cry because of their taskmasters; I know their sufferings, and I have come down to deliver them out of the hand of the Egyptians, . . . Come, I will send you to Pharaoh that you may bring forth my people (Exod. 3:7-8, 10)." Do you see the strangeness of those words; and yet, strange though they be, do you catch the significance of them? "I have determined to free my people. You go and do it for me." Well, that is the eternal pattern which God uses in relationship to his people and the establishment of his dream. He does not accomplish this on his own; he waits until we are willing to do it with him, until we allow him to work through us. Or to put it in another frame of reference, he calls us his partners. There is a trust basic to partnership that knows no limits. A partner really has no defense against the actions of his partner. Each can bind the other, and the other's assets. It is a high honor when God calls us his partner. And such we are. Jesus uses a different phrase. He says, "No longer do I call you servants, for the servant does not know what his master is doing; but I have called you friends, for all that I have heard from my Father I have made known to you (John 15:15)." It is to such a relationship that God calls us.

Now, a little more concerning this mission to which we are called. Its purpose is to fulfill the needs of men— all the needs of men: spiritual, physical, social. In fact, the needs of people cannot even be divided this way. And it is a lack of understanding of this indivisibleness that has involved the church so deeply in controversy these days. It is so easy for us to forget that a need is a need— and, as I heard it expressed one day, our bodies and our minds are so close together that they catch each other's diseases. In the epistle of James this is recognized so fully. The writer says, "If a brother or sister is ill-clad and in lack of daily food, and one of you says to them, 'Go in peace, be warmed and filled,' without giving them the things needed for the body, what does it profit (Jas. 2:15-16)?" Now, mark it well that those are not my words or the words of some modern prophet of the 1970's. Those are the words that were written long years ago. A need is a need, and God wants the needs met, whether they be needs of the body or of the spirit.

Not too long ago I was invited to a church to try to bring a little understanding of the stance of the United Church and its program of ministry. The man who led in the discussion kept saying that the church ought only to be interested and concerned about the spiritual needs of people. Finally, admitting the church's responsibility for the spiritual welfare of people, I asked him what he was going to do with these words of James and he had no answer. Of course, the church must be concerned about the spiritual needs of men—but the church must also respond in Christ's name to the physical needs of men: food, clothing, shelter, justice, employment. Or to put it differently, there is not one area of men's lives that is not the concern of God and of his Christ, and, therefore, of the church. The church must be concerned with the whole man. That is the mission. Not more concerned with his body than his spirit, but not less concerned either. Or to express it in a different fashion, the church is concerned with everything that affects a man or a woman or a child for good or ill, that makes his life more abundant or less abundant, that helps or is a stumbling block.

The church is concerned about people, and the church is concerned about people because God is concerned about people—against that which enslaves and for that which ennobles. So much for this. This is the mission to which all of us are called. Thank God all of us are called. It is the only hope there is—if all of us respond wholly to that call; for the need is so great and the extent so far-reaching that a few of us are as nothing against the problems and the dire needs.

He not only calls us, but also gives us his church. And what at heart is the church? It is the company of those who are committed to the mission—it is the fellowship of the concerned—it is the family of God. And why are we called to the church—why not each of us go out on our own? The answer to that seems simple to me. First of all, it is so much easier to do what is right and needed in the company of other people. I think this is made so plain when one watches a child. When the going is rough and the way is hard, the child often shrinks back until the mother says she will go along, and then the child goes eagerly and gladly. We are something like that. Let me use a very homely illustration. One of the newest expressions of this are Weight Watcher clubs. People are able to take pounds off much more easily in such a club than they are alone, even though all they read and all they hear is meant to impress them with the need of staying thin. All of us need the company of others committed so that we can keep our resolutions and promises strong.

We need also the spiritual nurture which we receive mainly through the church. The teaching function of the church is very important, the training which we receive in group discipline and group therapy. I remember that the one and only Halford Luccock wrote about the woman who said she would not have much trouble living the Christian life if it were not for that "little Jones boy" next door. Well, life always has its little Jones boy, and we become accustomed to and have some practice in the kind of large-heartedness which the Jones boy requires of us when we live within the framework of the church.

One of the great blessings of church life is that if it is a real church of our Lord, then everyone is welcome—or ought to be. The church is one place where if we are to be true to our faith we must get along with each other. Most of us need that kind of discipline. One of the values of going away to college (and I suppose to the army) is that one has to learn to tolerate other people. I would hate to think what kind of a world this would be if no one learned that lesson. For most people that is learned in the church—or it ought to be. If a man or a woman does not just suit my fancy, that is no reason why they should be excluded from the body of Christ. We are all children of God and therefore brothers one of another—and therefore we have to learn to get along together. This is the reason why it is tragic when people are excluded from a church because of race, or color or nationality or social status. And the people who are the losers are not the ones who are excluded, but the ones who do the excluding.

Enough of this. I want to add that the teaching function of the church—the inspiration which we ought to receive, the call to study the scriptures, the help in interpreting them, the chance to worship and celebrate the worth of our faith—all comes through the church and makes the church an important part of our practice of the Christian faith.

Then there is the very power which we can exert through the church. The church, like every social group, is more than the sum of its parts and exerts an influence far beyond what we could or would exert as people alone. Against the problems of our day we need all the clout which we can muster. I do not want to be pessimistic—but the truth is, when evil is organized as it is today (and for that matter as it always has been), one man standing for the right would be hard put to it to make an impact upon society for the right. The fact is that the outlook is so discouraging that many people voice the opinion to me that it is useless to try. In the church we have some extras going for us. We have the promise, "I will build my church, and the powers of death shall not prevail against it (Matt. 16:18)." We have the example of the apostles, who had nothing going for them that we would count important; but within the church they more than matched the power of the Roman Empire. You don't have to go back further than the Civil Rights Act of 1964 to find both the friends and the enemies of the legislation saying, "If it had not been for the church, the act would never have been passed." All I am trying to say is that through the church we can do together what we never could have done alone. And in these days of such gigantic problems, when some men suffer so much and others have so much, we need the unity of the church to make our voice—the voice of God and of his Christ—effective.

But there is more to it than this—much more. This is that the power of God is made available to us through the church. And how we need that power! Remember the promises: "Go therefore and make disciples of all nations, baptizing them in the name of the Father and of the Son and of the Holy Spirit, teaching them to observe all that I have commanded you; and lo, I am with you always, to the close of the age (Matt. 28:19-20)." The power of God is made available through his church. In every age the church has demonstrated with greater or lesser clarity what a few devoted but common people—one-talented people like us—can do when they have allowed God to work through them. This is the ever-recurring miracle which God works through his church. It is working now, if we give him a chance, and it will continue to work.

I have traveled up and down this country and in foreign lands, a total of well over a million miles. I have visited churches in open country, in small towns, in metropolitan cities. I have seen our missionaries at work, healing, teaching, demonstrating the way to live more abundantly, and I have seen this unchanging law of God at work everywhere. People who alone could never do

118

anything of worth have become servants of the living God empowered by his strength to do his will. It is one of the unending miracles of our faith and of our world that you and I can have a part in bringing God's dream to fruition. I shall never get done thanking God for his great gifts to us—his mission and his church.

CHAPTER 14
HE
GIVES US
ETERNAL LIFE

Jesus said, "I am the resurrection and the life; he who believes in me, though he die, yet shall he live, and whoever lives and believes in me shall never die (John 11:25)." "And this is eternal life, that they know thee the only true God, and Jesus Christ whom thou hast sent." He said, "Because I live, you will live also." The Statement of Faith expresses it this way: "He promises to all who trust him, forgiveness of sin and fullness of grace, courage in the struggle for justice and peace; his presence in trial and rejoicing and *eternal life in his Kingdom which has no end.*" Paul wrote, "For we know that if the earthly tent we live in is destroyed, we have a building from God, a house not made with hands, eternal in the heavens (2 Cor. 5:1)." God gives us eternal life. It is the contention of this chapter that this gift tells us as much about God as it does about man, or more.

Eternal life—God's gift to those who trust in him. That is the reason why we can be sure, why we need not doubt, why there is an affirmative answer to Job's question: "If a man dies, shall he live again?" If I were dependent upon what I do, what I can contrive upon my own merit for this eternal life, then for the life of me I never could be sure. But we are not dependent upon ourselves for eternal life, upon what we do, but rather upon the love and mercy of God. And his love and mercy are steadfast, they endure forever.

Eternal life—there is more to it than a life without end, though it does include that to be sure. It is qualitative as well as quantitative. If a man's life is founded on eternal principles, eternal truth, then what can "change and decay" do to that life? Nothing—for righteousness, truth, love, and faith stand forever. The burden of the teaching of Jesus about the kingdom and eternal life was that it abided forever because it was built upon and consisted of those things that are untouched by time and decay. For instance, eternal life—whether we are living it on Main Street in this year of our Lord or in some other time and place—is built upon love. Paul testifies that "Love bears all things, believes all things, hopes all things, endures all things. Love never ends (1 Cor. 13:7-8)." Well, if the foundation of the good life is made out of eternal stuff, in what danger can the superstructure stand? All this cannot be stressed too much!

Too many people associate eternal life only with life after what we call death. But the implied and direct teaching of Jesus was that a man can be (and ought to be) living eternally here and now. And he can, if he will build upon the eternal qualities of life and direct his days to that end. Of course, if a man will have nothing to do with that which abideth forever, it is not likely that he can expect to abide forever. It depends on the direction in which we build our day.

Let each man take care how he builds upon it. For no other foundation can anyone lay than that which is laid, which is Jesus Christ. Now if any one builds on the foundation with gold, silver, precious stones, wood, hay, stubble—each man's work will become manifest; for the Day will disclose it, because it will be revealed with fire, and the fire will test what sort of work each one has done.

—1 Corinthians 3:10-13

Faith is another eternal quality. For a man of faith there is no defeat or disaster. Trouble, yes; but the trouble is not devastating. We can rise above it. Another quotation of Paul comes quickly to mind:

> For we were so utterly, unbearably crushed that we despaired of life itself. Why, we felt that we had received the sentence of death; but that was to make us rely not on ourselves but on God who raises the dead; he delivered us from so deadly a peril, and he will deliver us; on him we have set our hope that he will deliver us again.
>
> —2 Corinthians 1:8-10

Just here the contrast which Paul uses in 2 Corinthians 5:1 is helpful. "For we know that if the earthly tent we live in is destroyed, we have a building from God, a house not made with hands, eternal in the heavens." The contrast is between living in a tent and living in a building of God. One is meant to be temporary and passing; but the other is meant to abide forever—sufficient for our every need. Begin now (or it is hoped that you began long ago) building a life that is beyond the reach of the earthy and earthly decay.

The other half of this promise has to do with life after death. Here scripture and our Lord are strangely silent concerning the details of that life. But he is not silent concerning the certainty of such a life. Prophets and poets have used the finest, most abiding, most precious materials to describe life in the other world. They wrote about golden streets and pearly gates and cities foursquare, harps, angels with halos, and great periods of rest. I fault them not for that (though I am left a little cold by it), because anyone is hard put to contrive such a description. What they were trying to do was to use the most extravagant description they knew. That what they thought was best is not what I think to be the most precious does not bother me too much. I can substitute my imaginings for theirs. I am sure, however, that the reality is far beyond these feeble delineations, either mine or theirs. Go back to what you have learned about God in these studies. How much greater, how much more wonderful is he than we once imagined! Remember the gifts he has given to us up to now. Can we doubt him who has provided for us so much more "than we can ask or think," to say nothing about what we deserve? Shall not he, with all these gifts, take us to himself in the life beyond our dying? Is it logical to believe that he who has brought us to this point, to this hour, will leave us in the end, desolate, alone, forsaken? He himself says, "I will not leave you desolate; I will come to you (John 14:18)." The much-beloved hymn "Lead, Kindly Light" says what I believe is truth:

> So long thy power hath blest me,
>   sure it still will lead me on
> O'er moor and fen, o'er crag and torrent,
>   till the night is gone;
> And with the morn
>   those angel faces smile
> Which I have loved long since,
>   and lost awhile.

I am satisfied to trust God and his presence with me and in me and to know that such companionship—whether before or after death, on earth or in heaven—will be good by any standards that have eternal worth.

The other day a friend asked concerning some of the details of eternal life. I replied that the Bible is very obscure concerning those details (though it is not obscure concerning the reality of eternal life). I continued that as for me, I am certain that, like all the other good gifts which God gives to his children, eternal life will be finer

123

and more splendid than the best we know. As Paul wrote: "For I know whom I have believed and I am sure that he is able to guard until that Day what has been entrusted to me (2 Tim. 2:12)."

God is the great giver: he gives us eternal life. What a great God we worship! We learn about him as we contemplate his great gifts.

THE
CONCLUSION
OF THE MATTER

Remember that the premise with which we began is that learning about God is not an end in itself, the goal of all our striving. Knowing him is of worth only if it helps us to see in what direction he is going and motivates us to go in that same direction after him. We are not expected ever to be "good for nothing" but to be "good for something." If, after you have read this book and contemplate in your own mind and heart the kind of a God that we have and you are no different from before, then the book, your time, and your effort are a waste. Such a book as this one has no purpose at all except to fit one for more useful and sacrificial service to the world and to the people in it—particularly to the people in it.

At the beginning I wrote that my concern today is that so many people are going out into the world to serve without having a faith and a knowledge to make them useful—down in the places where life is lived and where burdens ought to be lifted. But I have an equally important concern that having fit themselves with a faith and a knowledge, they will not put that faith and knowledge to work in a constructive way. These two concerns are not antithetical but complementary. Neither stands by itself alone. Without the other each is a dismal and tragic failure.

I must confess that just as there are congregations and peoples in those congregations that put too little stress on spiritual nurture, Christian education, learning about God, so there are also many congregations and people who do not put to work that which they already know. A congregation, a people, a person who is not on mission (God's mission) is of no worth and must be a stench in the nostrils of God himself. We were meant for mission as a fire is meant for burning. But the fire must be fed with fuel—and this book is devoted to pointing the direction from whence that fuel comes. Fuel and burning are equally important. One without the other is waste of the worst kind.

So do not quickly judge these words to be of no use, for they are pointed in the direction of nurture, increasing faith and understanding, and are not delineating the tremendous problems of our world and its people.

The purpose here is not to delineate a stern challenge to people to "get out where the action is," but rather to help them to get ready to go out.

The world must be made over. The old foundations are crumbling, the superstructure is falling. But only they will be able to make any lasting contribution to the rebuilding of the world who know for what the world was created, who is the Creator, what his purposes are, and how every man fits into that purpose. It is to trace a few guidelines in that study that this book was written.

We have a great God, and that God calls us to know him and then to go forth to transform life from what it is to what he means it to be. God keeps calling to mission. Be ready, eager, and fit to answer that call.

THE LIFE OF
BEN MOHR HERBSTER
Pastor—Preacher—Leader

Ben Mohr Herbster was the first president of the United Church of Christ, formed in June 1957, with 1.7 million members.

Small Town Roots. Born in the farm country of central Ohio on August 26, 1904, the son of a hardware merchant and a mother active in church work, Herbster grew up in the staunch faith and discipline of the Reformed Church, which remained with him the rest of his life. He graduated from the public schools in his hometown of Prospect and spent his college years at Heidelberg, some fifty miles away from home. During those years he indulged his love for debating, which was, perhaps, a harbinger of his later love of preaching.

In 1926 Herbster went to Dayton to enroll in the Central Theological Seminary, later merged into the present Eden Seminary. He graduated in 1929 and was ordained in the Reformed Church in the U.S.A. Shortly after graduation, he married Elizabeth Beam. His first pastorate was a missionary church, the Corinth Boulevard Reformed Church in Dayton, where he served for two years.

Cincinnati Pastorate. In 1931 Herbster accepted a call to the Zion Reformed Church in Norwood, a suburb of Cincinnati, where he and Elizabeth remained for thirty years.

Herbster saw his ministry as a dual responsibility — preaching and pastoring. Sunday mornings were spent in the pulpit delivering the sermons he had carefully crafted during the week. As a pastor, he was continually responsive to the needs of his parishioners. Day or night he answered calls and stayed as long as needed.

While at Zion he was instrumental in forming "Missions, Inc.," the predecessor organization of the present Cincinnati Assembly. This group organized mission churches and assisted community organizations. Herbster's recognized ability to "get people to do things" and his management talents brought him increasing responsibility.

Evangelical and Reformed Church. Herbster took part in the discussions that brought the Reformed and Evangelical denominations together into the Evangelical and Reformed Church in 1934. He served as president of the Cincinnati Council of Churches and president of the Southwest Ohio Synod of the Evangelical and Reformed Church. He also chaired the Ohio Pastor's Convention.

A strong supporter of the importance of an enlightened, local church as a basic unit to carry on the work of Christianity, he was committed to racial justice and Christian unity.

Ecumenicity. Deeply ecumenical in his outlook, Herbster was a leader among the Evangelical and Reformed ministry who pressed for the merger with the Congregational Christian Churches. He played a key role in the negotiations that led to the formation of the United Church of Christ. Avery Post, immediate past president of the UCC, described Herbster's role as "a theologian: a quiet, resolute man whose pastoral and diplomatic skills made him the perfect individual to knit together the diverse and often complicated elements in the United Church of Christ."

During one trying period when it seemed that merger would never occur, Herbster was leader of a devotional service for those involved in the negotiations, which is credited "with keeping the flame alive," leading to eventual success.

The proposed merger of the Congregational Christian Churches and the Evangelical and Reformed Church was agreed to in June 1957. The merger represented the first time in American religious history that two bodies from distinctly different backgrounds and church polities were united to form a single church. The denomination today is considered one of the most progressive in mainline Protestantism.

United Church of Christ Presidency. Ben was elected the first president of the United Church of Christ at its constituting General Synod in 1961, and he was reelected to a second four-year term in 1965.

According to Post, "Dr. Herbster was determined that the new church he helped form would be dedicated to carrying out the biblical directive to be the servant of the poor, the ill, the unjustly imprisoned and the dispossessed people of the world."

United Church Homes. Herbster was elected to the board of trustees of United Church Homes, Inc. in 1971. He chaired the statewide church campaign that raised the funds to build Trinity and other expansions of United Church Homes.

Ben Herbster also served on the United Church Homes Finance Committee, where he soon became aware of the need for annual support funds to provide benevolent care to under-financed residents of all United Church Homes retirement communities. This support is given through the benevolent care ministry known as "The Life Enrichment Fund."

Within the Trinity Community, he served on two residential study committees that resulted in the construction of two four-cottage units. After their construction, he and his wife moved into one of them in 1981. Elizabeth Herbster still resides at Trinity.

Revered Leader. Ben Mohr Herbster died on December 16, 1984. At the memorial service, Avery Post described Ben Herbster as "a Christ-centered and people-focused pastor, rooted in the Word of God, the integrity of his motives, his love and care for people, and his stubbornness to do right, whatever the cost."

The church remembers its first president as "a great preacher, pastor, administrator, and leader of the United Church of Christ . . . Ben M. Herbster, a servant of the Lord."